13 Ways Going on a Field Trip

Trip

Spotted Toad

ISBN-10: 1519041918
ISBN-13: 978-1519041913

1 Igneous, Sedimentary, Metamorphic

When I first started teaching, I lived in Washington Heights, right underneath Fort Tryon Park's huge hill. The neighborhood was then a mix of Dominican and Orthodox Jewish families, some of whom had connections with Yeshiva U. I found out later that my grandmother, though not Orthodox, had lived within a few blocks of my apartment half a century before me, right after she reached the United States, not long after she had walked off a Nazi transport disabled by an Allied bombing run, shrapnel still in her breast.

I was teaching 6th grade Life Science (2 classes), 7th grade Physical Science (2 classes), and 8th grade Earth Science (2 classes). I knew the least about Earth Science, so I spent the most time thinking about it.

Every weekend day, and some days after school, I would climb up the hill to Fort Tryon and go walking along the path beneath the Cloisters Museum, looking out over the Hudson, and thinking about how the water had carved out the rock I was standing on, how the river and its valley had been formed not too long ago, most likely when people were already living nearby, and how the rock itself– jagged, shiny, folded into swirling shapes, was old, older than mammals or birds.

In the end, we are all pushed around by forces bigger than ourselves.

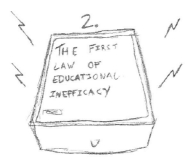

2 THE FIRST LAW OF EDUCATIONAL INEFFICACY

When I started teaching, I had a noisy and boisterous 7th grade class as my homeroom (I also taught them science). We were told, in the before-the-school-year meeting for all teachers, that homeroom– which in theory lasted from 8:40 to 9:00, but in practice went from whenever the kids finished at their locker until the bell rang at 9:03 and the attendance sheet was picked up– was for silent reading, and only silent reading. So a few kids would show up at 8:32, sit at their desk, get out their silent reading book, and start reading The Giver or the Life Story of Derek Jeter or whatever, but within a few seconds another louder kid would come in, or slam their locker outside, or stand outside the room eating a bacon-egg-and-cheese from the bodega across the street, until all the kids who had been reading would explain that they hadn't eaten hardly anything for breakfast and gosh were they hungry, and finally the more wiseguy kids (who knew we weren't allowed to mark them late until 9:00 on the dot) would stroll in right before the bell, glancing contemptuously at those poor suckers still clinging to their assigned reading book, and comment how good the bacon-egg-and-cheese had been. While I, inexperienced and inefficacious, was more incompetent at keeping my homeroom reading than most of the teachers in the school, it was clear I was hardly alone, since within a week or two the principal would come on the loudspeaker and demand "SILENCE FOR SILENT READING," several times a morning, which had the few remaining literateurs looking up in dismay, wondering if they were in trouble and if they hadn't been silently reading silently enough, and only gradually getting back to their books.

Meanwhile, however, the school– a hulking yellow overcrowded block of cinderblock that squatted on its South Bronx hillside like a Vogon spaceship demolishing the Earth– had decided that it was going to disintegrate into Small Learning Communities. Small Learning Communities– theme-based schools-within-a-school where a group of teachers would teach a common group of students and even follow them across the grades– were all the rage then, and so big signs were hung on each floor– "Media and Communications," "Professions and Careers," "Performing and Visual Arts," and so on, as the theme for the new schools-within-a-school. Almost immediately, Media and Communications realized that they needed to be producing Media, so the obvious implication was made and a different group of kids from the third floor would trot down to the Main Office every morning and start producing Media over the loudspeaker: reading the weather report, announcing birthdays, giving shout-outs to their friends. A generally good time, but the last straw for the few kids trying to learn the details of Derek Jeter's 1997 season, who would resignedly look up at the loudspeaker, their face in their palm, and listen. Even this was not consistent, however, since occasionally the group of kids from the third floor wouldn't be sent down in time, so instead we'd get "SILENCE FOR SILENT READING" just when we were waiting for the weather report.

This is the First Law of Educational Inefficacy: Any Educational Agenda will Cause an Equal-and-Opposite CounterAgenda to be Formed. The Agenda and CounterAgenda mingle, interact, make noise, and then dissipate in a cloud of photocopied handouts.

3 SECTION SHEETS

The neighborhood of the first school I taught in, a middle school in the south Bronx, was already majority black and Hispanic when the school was built in the early 60s. The classroom I taught in would, in the school's early days, have been an impressive place to learn science, a huge room with sinks and gas lines all around the perimeter and a huge demonstration table at the front. But times change. By the time I got there in 2000, the gas lines had long ago been permanently shut off. The faucets were hacked off at the base, leaving jagged pieces of metal coming out of the lab benches. The sinks were choked with debris and, in some cases, emptied not into plumbing but directly into the cabinet below, so that when young Jose and Arthur tried out their model volcano, a flood of baking soda-and-vinegar lava coursed across the floor. The chemical cabinets were empty, except for decades of old dittos and worksheets, several nests of mice, and one unstoppered bottle of concentrated hydrochloric acid, the fumes of which had gradually made the locker that held it as full of rusty metallic dust as the canyons of Mars.

I had two worst days teaching in the Bronx. The second, I'll get to some other time. The first was a Friday before a long weekend in February, my first year, and I had just about gotten through 8th period with my insane homeroom class, 7-221.

You called the groups of kids by their grade and their homeroom number, even though they moved around the building from class to class all day: 6-229 and 6-231, 8-215 and 8-217, 7-211 and 7-221 were my six classes. My homeroom was insane because they were my homeroom, and the homeroom teacher had chief responsibility for disciplining their class, even if (as in my class) they saw me mostly for a few minutes in the beginning and end of the day, along with a random splatter of science in the weekly schedule, and spent most of the day in math and reading. It was still your responsibility as homeroom teacher to keep them in line.

The school's main discipline system was the Section Sheet. Every day, a kid was picked to carry around a photocopied worksheet from class to class, and at the end of the period the teacher would give the class a grade from 1 to 5 and write some kind of comment in the box, like "2: Joey and Jose throwing paper balls," or "4: Talkative but good work!" and so forth. Then it would be the responsibility for the homeroom teacher to grill Joey and Jose, or call their parents, or get the floor dean Mr. Melman involved who would bring them into his office to grill them or call their parents.

It was all shadowboxing, of course, getting their parents mad enough for the kids to be a little scared but not so mad that they hit the kid or punished them badly enough that they came in sullen and angry for the rest of week or month or year. Calling a kid's house for misbehavior worked the first time, mostly, a little, and stopped working soon thereafter. Calling a kid's house for improvement instead of misbehavior worked beautifully on most kids but was dangerous– if you made a "good call" and then the kid didn't get a good grade at the end of the quarter, the parent would, reasonably enough, be pissed.

In any case, you were supposed to go through a bunch of rigamarole with your homeroom and the Section Sheet at the end of the day. "Shantae: not participating in gym class! I'm disappointed. Franklin: hitting in the line at the end of reading? I think I'm going to have to call home, what do you think?" If the homeroom teacher was sufficiently fearsome or morally authoritative, the threat of merely writing the name down on the section sheet in another class would inspire terror; for several years I kept an audio tape of my class I made one day, where for a few minutes all you hear is inaudible background chatter and a piercing voice repeatedly screaming, "DON'T WRITE DOWN MY NAME!"

I, of course, didn't have that kind of fearsomeness or moral authority. I had lost a good deal of credibility from the very first day, when seventh grade was called down to the auditorium and the names of kids by homeroom teacher were called. Everyone wanted Mr. F., a fat, funny, foul-mouthed English teacher who looked like a 6'3" version of The Penguin. I had grown a beard that summer and wore a tweed jacket in a misplaced desire not to look 21 (Youth, wasted on the idiotic young, I tell you), and Shanequa took one look at me standing along the wall of the auditorium and said what everyone was thinking: "Cornball." When thirty-one names were called for my class instead of Mr. F.'s, there was a long and audible groan that spread across the rows of seventh graders before they got up and lined up behind me.

I brought my class back to room 221, the cavernous but dysfunctional science lab I had been assigned; I assigned them seats by passing out index cards with seat numbers on them and called the roll. The class was cheering up after the disappointment of not being in Mr. F.'s class, snickering when Kwame told me I should call him Kwe or Danny told me I should call him DJ, and filling out the emergency contact cards I had left on each sheet. This was school– boring and pointless enough, but after a whole summer of not seeing each other, it was a bit of fun just to be back and see what happened next.

What happened next was Floyd DaCosta. I had been warned about Floyd– Mrs. Ackerman, the gnomish 6th grade math teacher next door, had scanned her wizened finger down my homeroom list: "loud, loud, sweet, smart, loud, oh you've got Floyd." But when I called roll he wasn't there, though his birthday was, a good seventeen years and change before the date he was supposed to show up in seventh grade and learn to care about solving proportion problems and reading Rikki-Tikki-Tavi. I marked the bubble next to his name in the ATS scantron attendance sheet: absent. Right afterwards, he came in through the classroom door, taller than me (or Mr. F.), long braids and do-rag, no bookbag but a mechanical pencil behind his ear. All the kids– most of them twelve, with a few thirteen year olds, two fourteen year olds, and one sixteen-year old in there– looked up from filling out the emergency cards as he strolled into the room, ignoring my proffered index card with his assigned seat, and sat down in an unoccupied seat in the back. Everyone watched Floyd to see what would happen next.

"What, all eyes on me?" he said, in a deep bass-baritone. Everyone pretended to look at their emergency cards again.

"'sup, Floyd," said Precious, the sixteen-year-old.

"School," he said in disgust, and closed his eyes as if to close out the indignity of being in this little-kid class, and kept them closed until the bell rang for everyone to get up and go to their next period. Then the PA turned on– "will all teachers please hold their homeroom class for an additional period until the student schedules are ready." We all sat down, and I passed out the work I had been planning for the first science period. Then, the PA came on and told us to keep our class for another period, and I tried to teach the lesson about the scientific method I had vaguely planned for the next day. "Problem, Hypothesis, Experiment, Results, Conclusion," I said. Floyd got up and walked out.

Franklin- a fine-featured Dominican kid with a timid voice- raised his hand. "Can I carry the Section Sheet?" Someone had explained the section sheet to me, but I didn't really get the importance kids placed on it. "Sure," I said, and went to hand it to him. "You should get a folder for it, so it doesn't get ripped," some kids yelled. "Don't give it to Franklin! He's bad." "You should write down that Floyd walked out of the class." I gave Franklin the sheet, which he placed ceremonially into an empty folder and held like a sacred chalice in front of him while he got in line to go to the next class.

Floyd turned out to be the least of my problems. He barely showed up after the first day, and when he came he was quiet. He'd sit down, pretend to do a few questions on whatever worksheet or whatever we were doing, then walk out a few minutes before the end of the period, so he wouldn't have to line up with the little kids. It was insane that he was there, just like it was insane that Precious and Heriberto (the other 16-year-old seventh grader, in the other homeroom) were there, not-learning the same three paragraph essay formats and American History dates they hadn't learned three or four times before. But we wrote down grades for him, until one day he disappeared from the ATS attendance sheet– locked up or transferred to a special school, there were different stories– and he was someone else's problem.

In any case, I had two hundred other problems– six science classes, with the two sixth grade classes so big (40 and 42 respectively) that several kids carried their desks with them from class to class. It wasn't just my cornballishness that stopped me from keeping my homeroom in line: it was my science class. The section sheet system worked fine if every class had a roughly equal incidence of misbehavior, so that the burden was balanced across homerooms. But my science class, especially in the two 7th grade Physical Science sections, was an explosion of adolescent energy and lab station matter from day one. The electrolysis of water experiment led to washing soda on the ceiling and old vinegar coursing across the floor. Meanwhile, my experiences working in schools in Philadelphia two years before were of little avail to me, since I was totally unprepared for organizing three different subjects for two hundred kids. I couldn't even handle the section sheet- I'd be writing on one of the flip-chart pads I hung around the room with a Magic Marker (my chalkboard handwriting proved too illegible for anything but emergencies) when a paper ball, then another, then another would pass across the room, as an impromptu demonstration of kinematics. I'd cast around for the section sheet-where was it where was it- and when I finally found it, scribble down the names of the probably offenders in Magic Marker, which just added to the general note of ridiculousness of my class when it came time for Ackerman or F. or Williams or any of the other teachers with a clue what they were doing to review the sheet at the end of the day.

But back to 8th period that Friday in February, lo these many years ago. Everyone knows the week, and the school day, have their own rise and fall dynamic, like a Mahler symphony or a Led Zeppelin show. Monday's child was sour of face, mad to be back in school; Tuesday through Thursday you could get some work done; Friday's child was in a frenzy at the prospect of getting out of there. Same with 8th period. 7-221 would tear in from 7th period gym, straggling up the stairs, all red in the face from dodgeball or steal the bacon, first Jeffrey, then DJ, then Janeris, rushing in and sprawling on the nearest seat at hand, huffing and puffing, then demanding to go get some water from the hall. At first I tried to reel it in, one kid then the next, each with a semi-official hall pass going down to the water fountain, leering at Senor Hernandez's bilingual class next door, then slowly sauntering back. But the kids would all claim to have asthma (this was the South Bronx, so it wasn't that implausible) and that they were going to have an attack if they didn't get some water right away. Then, I gave up and lined everyone up to take them to the water fountain, where everyone acted like Chevy Chase in the Three Amigos, and by the time we got back the class was halfway over, at which time Arthur would finally show up from gym, bouncing his basketball once, twice between his legs and shoots off the the wall over the blackboard. Around December, I gave up teaching any kind of real lesson Fridays 8th period (forgive me, Teach for America, for I have sinned) and would pass out some science vocabulary crossword puzzles or other busywork and walk around joking and glowering at them if they threatened not to write down that _ _ _ _ _ _ _ : Mass/Volume wasn't density, or whatever.

It was still touch and go, but that Friday I was sure I was in the clear. The bell was soon to ring, the three-day weekend was so close I could taste it, and I told everyone to line up.

Franklin had, in fact, turned out to be a terrible Carrier of the Section Sheet. Despite his angelic demeanor that first day, he was constantly and near-silently telling other kids the precise words that would drive them absolutely bonkers. Johnson, the inclusion kid with a zeroth-grade reading level, was his most frequent target, but everyone would come in for it sooner or later, and howl with rage before striding over to him to wrest the section sheet from his hands in hope of scribbling down his name ("since you don't do nothin anyway!" with an accusatory finger at me) on the sheet.

On the day in February, Danny D. (not the other Danny, DJ, Danny J.) and he had lined up with the rest of the kids tapping their feet in anticipation of the three day weekend just like me, when boom! Franklin had whispered something unforgivable to Danny and Danny was on top of him on the floor, arms flying.

Let's pause the tape right there, as I was hauling Danny off of Franklin, and observe that for all the craziness in that school (the school was threatened with State Takeover that year and was put under State Supervision the following year) roughly none of the boys had expressed any interest in hurting each other up to that point. Some chest bumping, some growling, some yells of "Hold me back! Hold me back!" and then they were only too happy for you to hold them back. The girls were a different story, as one wild hair-pulling incident between Irina and Sanjida had revealed, but the boys only wanted to be seen to be eager to fight, not to do it.

But let's unpause the videotape. I pull Danny off of Franklin, hold him back underneath his arms, while Franklin stood up and with a look of cold determination, gave Danny a right cross (THUNK!) to his face while I held him back. I gaped, and let go of Danny, who coughed in shock and pain – it was an act of such (literal) underhandedness I was speechless.

The bell rang, and Franklin dashed out, followed by 7-221, abuzz with what just happened, followed by Danny, fat-lipped and eager for revenge. Mr. Melman, the dean, caught him at the door.

"Did you put what happened on the Section Sheet?" he said to me.

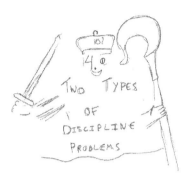

4 TWO TYPES OF DISCIPLINE PROBLEMS

You can (pretentiously) group classroom discipline problems under two headings: The Problem of Political Authority and The Phenomenology of Knowledge.

The Problem of Political Authority- Why should we do what the teacher says?

The Problem of Political Authority is what occurs to an observer, let's say the assistant principal, when she walks into a classroom where all the kids are yelling at each other, three kids are out of their seats staring out of the window, somebody's eating, and somebody's crying. Why doesn't the teacher do something? Don't they have any respect?

Teachers are quite limited in the formal means offered to them to get kids to do what they want: they can proffer grades or some more tangible sort of reward (popcorn party Fridays!), they can threaten to call parents or to exile kids to an administrator's room or to the back of the classroom, but they obviously can't make the kids do anything. Although teachers are often referred to as in loco parentis, this isn't actually true: a friend of mine teaching in another middle school had a parent of one of her students tell her that she would be coming in to give the kid a spanking in front of his peers– "I called the Health Department, and the law says I'm allowed to give him three claps on his behind," and though my friend dissuaded the parent from this unwise course of action, it did illustrate how parents are not teachers and school is not home.

So, instead, teachers must rely on implicit authority, the kids' desire for their approval or fear of their reprisal, or just the tendency, if everyone else is behaving, to go along to get along.

For schoolteachers as well as philosophers, the resolution to the Problem depends on assumptions about human nature in the absence of formal constraint. In the absence of authority, will school become a darkened pandemonium, a nasty and brutish war of all-against-all, or will pupils engage in mingled work and conversation and play, as light and harmless as the sun streaming in through the classroom window?

There are a number of books for teachers attempting to resolve The Problem of Political Authority. You can try Assertive Discipline (put kids' names on the board and then put checkmarks next them) or Positive Discipline (make the kids feel good and they won't misbehave) or the Responsive Classroom (an engaged democracy of learners is just around the corner). Many of these methods are useful, and will make everyone less crazy and miserable if followed with some finesse.

The Phenomenology of Knowledge

What is the teacher even talking about?

The Student in the Back Seems Disengaged...What Strategies Will You Employ to Differentiate the Lesson for Him?

A considerable number of classroom discipline problems arise not because the teacher is not charismatic enough, or assiduous enough in writing down names and putting checkmarks next to them, or calling homes for good behavior or bad, or engaging the kids in democratic decisionmaking and group process, and not because the students aren't at least theoretically enthusiastic about learning all that school stuff and making their parents proud, but because the students have no idea what is going on academically in the class at all. This may be a solvable problem, it may not be.

I went to visit the classroom of a young math teacher in Spanish Harlem once– a charismatic guy with incredible drive, who like many of his students, was a recent immigrant from the Dominican Republic. He clearly was working like a madman in the classroom and out to make his students love math and learn all the crazy problem solving techniques that the New York State 8th grade test was now testing. Most math teachers wave at "inquiry methods" on their way by and then go back to the old standbys of assigning problems and explaining how to solve them, but this guy put his money where his mouth was and made sure every single lesson involved group problem solving, use of math manipulatives, gradual introduction of new topics in algebraic reasoning by moving from the concrete to the representational to the verbal to the abstract.

An acquaintance ended up student teaching in this guy's class. She said he was great, the kids were great, they all loved his class, but the class ended up being complete madness half the time, because the kids were on a 3rd or 4th grade level and he was insisting on teaching them what they were supposed, according to the New York State Department of Education, to learn in 8th grade.

Some problems in the Phenomenology of Knowledge can be resolved by going slower, by teaching again what was not understood before, to do as this teacher did and develop carefully planned interactive lessons with a variety of materials. But some problems cannot be; the expectations of the planners of educational programs may just be too far afield, and the rest of us can never catch up.

5 HOME VISITS

I went on my first visit to a kid's house a few weeks before the fight between Franklin and Danny, my first year teaching. Lavonne was a big, muscular kid, 15 in the 8th grade, who would assiduously copy down whatever was on the board, his head leaning down over his notebook to make sure he got the letters right, a football held in his lap, and earnestly raising his hand high to answer whatever questions he knew the answers to. He lived in Harlem, unlike all the other kids (who lived in the school's immediate neighborhood in the Bronx), and while he certainly wasn't unique in living with his dad, he probably was unusual in expressing more fear of his father catching him out for not working at school or getting in trouble than of his mom. Then, sometime in December, he started getting in not-quite-fights every day as he entered or left the class, usually with Owen, a tall, lanky kid with a big smile and lots of jokes who was always getting in trouble (and the only genuinely talented basketball player among my students that year), also 15 and the only one of the 8th graders who might possibly been a fair fight for Lavonne. Lavonne would get up from his desk, carefully putting away his notebook and one of his treasured, fancy metal ballpoint pens, and Owen would swipe his football from his seat or tap his shoulder or create a distraction and then swipe one of the pens still on his desk, and then we'd have the usual "Hold me back, hold me back" and chest bumping of boys who have no real intention of fighting but don't want to make that too obvious. Eventually, Owen would just have to look in Lavonne's direction and Lavonne would get angry, standing up in the middle of class and creating uproar among the kids who were only too happy to stop copying from the board or making notes on the igneous and metamorphic rocks they were observing. (8th grade was Earth Science, and the curriculum I had the most trouble with .) It was Owen's fault, at some level, but blaming Owen for creating uproar was like blaming the ocean for knocking you down at high tide– it was just the way it was going to be.

I had tried holding Lavonne after class, moving his seat, writing his name on the Section Sheet, confiscating his football, but nothing made any difference; in any case, the phone number on his blue emergency card hadn't worked since September, and so I couldn't call his home. Then Lavonne threw over a desk in exasperation one day, and I decided it was time to try visiting his house. (Everyone lived in apartments, of course, but everyone equally called it their "house.") Home visits were one of the only techniques generally endorsed both by my 40-year-veteran colleagues and my 2-years-of-experience Teach for America program director– "when nothing works, showing up at their door'll put the fear of God into them," as Mr. Israel, the math teacher down the hall, had said.

I lived not too far from the address on his blue card, and that Sunday I went down from Washington Heights to east 147th street and rang his top floor bell. It was pouring rain, and I waited at the door for a few more minutes, soaked, when finally a voice from the intercom asked who it was. I said it was Lavonne's teacher from school, and they buzzed me in.

When I came in, Lavonne was perched on the armrest of a couch, next to at least six of his male relatives or neighbors, watching the NFL playoffs on a tiny color TV. It was raining inside the apartment. There were at least five buckets all over the quite large but dark and dank living room, and the rain was pouring down from the ceiling in almost continuous streams into them, as well as a few leaks that weren't being caught.

"We're having some trouble with our roof," Lavonne's dad said apologetically, as he came to the door with Lavonne's uncle, to shake my hand. Lavonne suddenly seemed like a tiny five year old boy, his eyes huge as he stared in terror from his perch on the couch. "Get away from that television set," Lavonne's uncle snapped back at him, and Lavonne stood up, uncertain whether he was supposed to come over to us, and just stood where he was, looking at his hands.

I explained the desk throwing, Lavonne having trouble controlling his anger.

"But Owen-" Lavonne interjected in a strangled voice.

"Shut it."

Lavonne's mom arrived, to hand me a working phone number to contact them with.

"Please contact us any time at all," his dad said. I apologized for disturbing their Sunday and went on my way, as someone added a sixth bucket to catch another leak.

The next day, Mr. Israel's second prediction– "they'll give you a bunch of free advertising afterward," came true: I walked past Lavonne's homeroom and he was with great melancholy recounting the story of the visit, "right in the middle of the football game!"

After that, I went on half a dozen visits in the next few months, whenever I couldn't reach parents on the phone: Franklin's mom seemed far too young to have a middle-school-aged son; Shanequa's grandmother(or great-grandmother?) was gracious but seemed very tired, the apartment neat and orderly but every surface seeming aged and worn; Eric's mom was as loud and boisterous as him, hugely obese in a wheelchair, the TV blaring behind her. And so on. There was only one home that seemed like it might have been unsafe; Samantha's mom had gone to back to the Dominican Republic for three months, leaving her in care of a high-school aged cousin, the kitchen and floor a disgusting mess. But I didn't call anyone higher up the chain of official trouble to report the place; at the time I figured if I was going to show up at these people's homes uninvited and unexpected, I should try not to invoke more than just a request to start behaving in my class.

It didn't make all the difference in the world, but it made a difference. Many of my problems were my own making– shouting too much and at the wrong times, losing the quizzes and never handing them back, the freakish piles of paper on the front desk and the illegible handwriting on the board. One day, I showed up for 5th period after my lunch break and "He makes home visits!" was written neatly in the corner of the board. It was a victory of sorts.

Near the end of the year, the principal- my perpetual adversary- had a mild heart attack and left the school for the rest of the year to recover. The next day, something undisclosed was discovered in the back staircase, and the vice-principal (and acting building principal) was called to the central district office to be held accountable. So two of the three administrators in the always-barely functional building were gone, and the halls became a highway of wandering kids all through the day, who'd wander it your room to scream "Wassup, West-Side!" and saunter away. Then, our state test scores came back, and we went from "in Danger of State Takeover" to "Under State Jurisdiction." This meant they automatically fired all teachers without tenure and then we had to reapply for our jobs.

When he told me I was getting rehired for the next year, the final remaining administrator, a youngish Caribbean guy with long dreads who always wore a dark suit, said, "this is for two reasons– first, that water rocket that you set off with Danny Jiminez in the middle of recess, which I thought was hilarious even though it didn't work, and second, because the kids all say you make home visits."

There were probably worse reasons he could have given.

6 PHILADELPHIA STORIES

Before I started teaching, I worked for a community service program in Philly for a year in the 90s. We had a wide cast of characters, sent to us by the foster system or the courts or recruited into the program on street-corners or in the mall, and most of them had funny stories about their teenage years (they had to be at least 18 to join the program, and they looked back upon their salad days, when they were green in judgment, with mingled amusement and regret.) The guy I worked closest with was Elijah/Ely (not his real name, of course, but appropriately Biblical), who was sent to us by a judge when he was kicked out of JobCorps, and looked like a more-handsome Chris Rock, with a Mephistophelean beard. He didn't have Chris Rock's range, but he had plenty of funny routines, particularly about the regret of a morning after drunkenness ("Oh please…God…please…I'll never drink again, Lord…please,") that I've thought about from time to regrettable time since then, as well as zombie-like impressions of the crackheads in the projects near Temple University where he had once lived. He invented an imaginary "Honorary Negro Card" he was going to bestow upon me, and would threaten me with stripping me of it were I to engage in undignified behavior like running for a city bus, and then re-bestowing it verbally when he saw me at a party talking with a young woman. Eventually– and shortly before he dropped out of the program– he handed me an enormous piece of purple construction paper appropriately made out and covered in Scotch tape in lieu of lamination, and with great ceremony said "Here it is."

In spite of numerous stories of fisticuffs and sexual exploits ("you ever walked off with a guy's girlfriend right after beating him in a fight?") he was in mild but continuous terror of his mom, with whom he still lived, and who had (like Pip's sister Mrs. Joe Gargery) brought him up "by hand," and he nursed a slyly encouraged but clearly unrequited love for the most voluptuous of our female colleagues. His most unbelievable story, but one repeated enough to have the air of truth, was that when he was fourteen years old he had earned enough money selling drugs to the crackheads that he and five of his friends went to a car dealership and bought a Plymouth Voyager with $22,000 in cash, which they drove around for a few weeks before crashing it and then getting it towed, never to be seen again. He invited me once to a New Year's Party at his house, and I was tempted to go, but then he kept saying how his neighbors would have to shoot off enough bullets to make the last two digits of the year (this was the 90s, remember), and I declined.

Midway through the year, my team got another young man sent from some vague run-in with the law, named Mike (well not really), and less agreeable. He was light-skinned and big, with incredibly long and well-manicured nails, and he spoke with a Tennessee Williams Southern drawl that seemed rather out of place with the allegations of fighting and f-ing everything that moved that were his regular conversation. He made the one girl on our team, a sweet-tempered and reliable person who had every indication of being headed to college until she got pregnant midway through the year, very uncomfortable, and gradually he also became what I thought a bad influence on Ely. Ely had always been somewhat unreliable– I had to call him up pretty much every morning if he was going to show up even close to on-time at one of the schools where we were tutoring or running community gardening projects– but when he showed up he had been cheerful and enthusiastic and his sense of humor was always a big hit with the kids, who were eager to be in his group in any activity. I was convinced that with my gentle harassment he was going to finish the program, get the small college scholarship that was attached, and move on with his life, or do another year in the program in a slightly more independent role. When Mike joined the team, though, soon he and Ely would excuse themselves to the bathroom around ten every morning and then reappear, high out of their minds, and useless for the rest of the day. Mike struck me as a bit of a sociopath– he could lie with less compunction than almost anyone I've ever known– and his time sheets were wall-to-wall fantasy, but he was persistent in his fabrications, but Ely was sufficiently honest to put down roughly correct hours on his time sheet, and he was clearly more-and-more behind where he needed to be if he was every going to finish the program. He stopped showing up one day, and when I saw him a few weeks later at someone's house, he said his mom was sending him to live with some relatives in the South.

(Eventually, Mike told me the story of how he had spent his teens in a group travelling from town to

town selling imaginary magazine subscriptions, going door to door tricking people into giving cash or credit cards that would pay for the subscription and give points towards an imaginary college fund, and staying in hotels with groups of kids and a few adults who took most of the money. This perhaps explained his facility at lying.)
Most of the young men ended up dropping out of the program before it finished, perhaps from Goffman-like troubles with the law but more likely because they kept not showing up and ran behind in hours, or had little pressure to bring home the meager paycheck since they were living at home either way. Most of the young women– even the many who got pregnant during the year– finished and got the scholarship. Many of them went to college, many of them moved up into program staff; one of them was the executive director of the program the last time I checked. The big patterns in social statistics are pretty often reflected in day-to-day life.

At one point, the whole program (all 90 or so of us) were shuffled off to SEPTA's headquarters to thank them for giving us free transit vouchers for the year and explain how we were going to be "SEPTA Ambassadors" as part of our year of service. Literally all of the governing executives of SEPTA were in the meeting, which was intended to be a light-hearted exchange of pleasantries but soon, once all my colleagues realized that these were the powerful people behind the transit system, devolved into a series of shouted denunciations of the 44 bus, which never comes on time, the Orange Line's track work and the broken steps to the El, which the SEPTA executives listened to with muted shock. Enlivened by the moment, I joined in to tell the suits in the room about the homeless guy I and a friend had found stabbed one morning at the 49th street Regional Rail stop.

When I became a teacher later, the year in Philly was a mixed blessing. Teaching is in many ways about setting expectations for kids and making some behavior seem impossibly out-of-bounds. While nothing can prepare you for the sheer noise of 35 out-of-control 7th graders, the general goofiness of my Philadelphia colleagues made all of the individual misbehavior of my students seem kind of droll, and my tendency was to be amused rather than appropriately outraged. That amusement made me stick-it-out longer, though, until I eventually became, by my own lights, a good teacher. So I owe Ely and Mike and the rest of the guys appreciation for that, wherever they may be.

7 SEEING AND SOLITUDE

When I was a kid, around nine years old, I realized
that if I told myself over and over to wake up early,
right before falling asleep, I would wake up in the
middle of the night. I tried it a few times, reducing the
intensity of my self-injunctions each time, and
eventually woke up just as the sun was starting to rise,
before the rest of my family was up. I crept down
from the finished attic I shared with my older brother,
out the door, and walked down the hill to the park a
few blocks from my house.

It was late May, and the lagoon in the park was green and covered with lilies; a family of ducks plopped from their nest into the water while I watched on the little bridge overhead. Painted turtles and muskrats swam in the water. The morning was noisy and busy and chirruping, but with no people.

I stayed for half an hour and then walked back up to my house. My dad, a perpetual early riser, was drinking coffee and reading the newspaper in the kitchen. He asked me what I had been doing and told me not to do it again.

A lot of what we call "being in nature" is in a way little more wild or dangerous than my 5 AM sojourn to the park when I was nine. When European explorers first reached the Grand Canyon, they turned back in disgust and dismay, calling it a barren wasteland. It was only after the railroad came, and the dangers of thirst and isolation were partially tamed, that it was determined to be a wonder of the world. And yet, like my brief view from the bridge of the birds and turtles and ducks, seeing what is there often requires a kind of attention that is best accomplished alone, at least a little ways away from other people.

Henry David Thoreau is often excoriated these days not just for being an insufferable know-it-all but for being not-so-self-reliant and not-so-isolated when he makes his famous experiment in isolated, self-reliant living. Walden Pond was then, as now, more-or-less nestled in the Boston suburbs, and Henry's mom would regularly bring him pies.

But I can't help feeling this misses the point, and not just because Walden is better read as poetry pretending to be polemic than as a straight-faced how-to guide.

Small children will watch, effortlessly and rapt, a beetle burrowing into the ground, froglets crossing a path, or a nest of ants scattering when a rock is overturned. In middle school, kids can still be tricked into paying attention, particularly for something gross or dangerous or illicit. By high school, the flicker of interest is for many kids vanished. As we age, the awareness of the social world often crowds out interest in the natural one, perhaps ever more so as the social world expands into vast electronic form.

My favorite Thoreau book, left now in a classroom somewhere, was a series of fragments from his journals opposite full-page photographs of leaves, rocks, clouds, a narrow stream or an abandoned nest. Seeing requires a sense of solitude, if not its truth, a willingness to push away for a moment our worries about who we are to other people to take in what is before our nose.

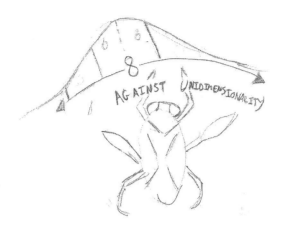

8 AGAINST UNIDIMENSIONALITY

During my mostly disastrous second year teaching in the Bronx, I worked on Saturdays at a state park about 50 miles north of the city, up the Hudson Valley. We would take classes of graduate teaching students up to the park, where they would look around for a research topic (spiders, oak trees, butterflies, etc) and then Do What Scientists Do, on the theory that if teachers felt more confident observing and studying living things themselves, they'd be more likely to help kids to do the same in their classrooms. (Urban elementary school teachers are in recent years notorious for not teaching science at all, to make room for all-reading-and-math, all the time.)

Whether it helped their teaching or not, tromping around after bugs or birds up in the Hudson Highlands was, on all but the rainiest Saturdays, great fun. One fall day, we climbed up a muddy hill and found a vernal pool entirely filled with chirruping frogs and their spawn. I brought a huge jar of them back to my classroom, hoping the kids could observe their tadpole-to-frog metamorphosis, but while many of the eggs hatched and became cute little tadpoles, there also happened to be a water boatman bug lurking in the jar as well, who despite being the same size as the tadpoles, ate them all up, one by one. One day, frustrated with his carnivory, I reached into the jar to grab him out; he bit me quite painfully and retreated to the other end of the jar. Nature red in tooth and claw.

The graduate teaching students in the classes were mostly an interesting bunch- often career changers who wanted a go at teaching in New York after trying social work, or banking, or law (or after securing a spouse with a higher-paying job.) One semester, we had a student who had just come back from a Peace Corps stint in Papua Guinea. I was reading Guns, Germs, and Steel then, and was struck by Jared Diamond's allegation, from his years doing ornithology in Papua New Guinea, that the residents of PNG were smarter than people elsewhere in the world. This didn't seem entirely unbelievable to me at the time, the idea that recent hunter gatherers might be just plain smarter than us settled-and-cizilized folks. My own middle school science classes seemed to be making their participants steadily stupider, for example. So I asked the recent Peace Corps returnee what she thought about New Guineans being extra smart.

"Well, they could make a shelter in the woods really well, and I can believe they were exceptionally good at helping Jared Diamond find birds and not get lost or killed in the jungle. But…" and then she told what she described as her 'classic Peace Corps development story.'

She and her husband were the only foreigners teaching at a remote public school. There wasn't any electricity at the school, or anywhere nearby, so her husband won a grant to purchase a generator and fuel, which he was hoping to use to run a refrigerator so they could store medicine and run a small clinic for the kids. Somehow, one of the (New Guinean) teachers brought in an ancient television set that still worked, and pretty soon, the refrigerator was constantly being unplugged (the generator didn't produce that much power) to allow for the TV to be plugged in to show endless reruns of Baywatch. The medicine was spoiled, and the other teachers began sleeping through their classes, because they had been up all night watching Baywatch.

"And that's how most Peace Corps development projects go," she finished.

It is possible to believe that IQ is a meaningful and reliably-measured construct, is largely inherited, is important for individual and group differences, and isn't identical to the meaning of the word "intelligence," whether for Papua New Guineans or for the rest of the world.

Ironically, teaching is a career that encourages this distinction, and not just because getting up in the morning and trying to get a group of fourteen-year-olds interested in mitochondria requires a degree of delusion and self-deception. It is both true that general cognitive ability is a hugely neglected explanatory factor for what goes on in schools and that, paradoxically, teaching is one of the careers in which IQ-the kids' and your own- can seem less important than you'd think. This is both because an ample IQ is of relatively little help in being a good teacher, especially in the short run, and because every day you're around dozens of kids who couldn't pass the end-of-year Algebra II test if their life depended on it but are, nonetheless, witty, insightful, curious people with whom you can have intellectually engaged conversations about the presidential election or the water boatman bug that just ate another tadpole.

In other words, abstraction and inference- which, at some level, is what IQ is about- isn't everything. This is true of the theoretical physicist who got entrapped by an obvious catfishing scam and ended up in a South American prison for drug trafficking, yearning for his imaginary internet girlfriend. And it's true for me, when I can't find my car in a parking lot, remember the lyrics to a pop song, or keep track of a piece of paper for more than a few hours. As my best friend said to me, when we were walking home from elementary school many years ago, "you're smart, but you're an idiot."

Perhaps the water boatman bug thought much the same thing.

9 HE DIDN'T DO NUTHIN

It's a ritual of middle school teaching I almost miss.

Something happens: a note is passed, a paper ball flies across the room, someone shouts out a joke when everyone is supposed to be quiet. The teacher fixes their gaze upon the likely suspect, who protests, in simulated or truthful innocence, "I didn't do nuthin'!"

To which, the kid sitting next to the accused says, in mournful affected disappointment, "that's right, didn't do nuthin'. You ought to have been doin' your work." And then, turning to the teacher and shaking his head dolefully, "I tell you, mister, these kids today."

In practice, of course, the accused kid very well may have been better off doin' nuthin' than doing his work. Doing your work means writing things down; in middle school at least, a practice that for many kids more-or-less assures that their full attention is focused on forming or copying letters rather than on the topic of discussion or relevant thoughts. For many kids, keeping them writing keeps them quiet enough to assure a simulacrum of learning in the classroom, but may at times prevent actual learning from taking place.

For teachers, too, doin' nuthin' is an underrated tack. Even the most dedicated reformist will generally concede that first year teachers are, on average, less effective than their more experienced colleagues. But, if truth be told, it is often because those first year teachers are doing too much rather than not enough: too much disciplining, too much lesson-planning, too much teaching, and none of it very well. The economists have a perfectly valid concept for this: negative marginal product, and while they usually ascribe it to a surplus of workers without enough capital to provide for them (if you gotta too many-a pizza cooks without-a enough counter space, you cannot make-a the pizza pie) it is equally coherent to talk about a within-worker diminishing or negative marginal product, hour-by-hour or minute-by-minute rather than employee-by-employee.

Almost anybody– even a halfway conscious assistant principal completing his fifth formal classroom observation of the day– can walk into a classroom and suggest something more the teacher could or should be doing. It is much harder- both technically and culturally— to tell someone to do less.

10. 9/11/01

When 9/11 happened, at the beginning of my second year teaching, I was administering a beginning-of-the-year standardized test to my 6th grade homeroom when the aide who was handing out the bubble sheets to all the classrooms told me someone had crashed a plane into the World Trade Center, and that there were reports of a second plane as well. The kids overheard the aide's words.

"Who crashed a plane, Mister?"

"Let's have a moment of silence," I said, pretty sure that was what I was supposed to do in these situations.

There were some uncomfortable giggles and a few restless seconds of silence, and then I kept handing out the bubble sheets.

I gave the test to the kids and waited while they filled it out. The next period was my "prep" (free period), and I went over to find Mr. F, one of my students' English teachers: a fat, funny, foul-mouthed former salesman and the teacher's union rep.

"Who did it?" I asked him. "Bin Laden?" (The USS Cole had been bombed just the year before.)

"Who the fuck knows?" Mr. F said. "Bin Laden says he wasn't involved. And there was another plane that just crashed into the Pentagon."

I went to go teach my next class.

Parents had begun arriving around 10AM to pick up their kids. By 11:15, the end of the next period, a long line of anxious parents snaked down the second-floor hallway, from the main office all the way to my classroom, waiting to be told where their child was. The main office called out name after name over the PA system, and the hallway became total confusion, as kids would wander out to go find their parents in the line, and other kids came from the first or third or fourth floors or the "movable classroom" trailers outside to find their parents. The school had a lot of trouble keeping kids in the right place under the best of circumstances.

Arthur and Jose, who were no longer in my homeroom but I still had in my 8th grade science class, raised their hands.

"They called my name."

"Mine, too."

Medjine, who was, to her great disgust, stuck in class with these two bozos for yet another year of middle school, shook her head.

"Mister, they didn't call their names."

Ooooh. Different kids called out. *Lyin to a teacher. Tryin to get out of class. Suspended the first week of school. We're very disappointed in you, young men.*

Now that it was a joke, about half the kids started raising their hands to say that their names had been called.

Finally, the PA stopped its endless list of students' names. Another approach was being tried. Teachers were told one by one to bring their classes down to the auditorium, where they marched past parents standing along the walls, who were supposed to point out their children like suspects in a lineup. Some more jokes– Shanequa said she saw her grandmother over on the other side of the auditorium, can she go, it's hard for her grandmother to see that far, and so on. With a sigh, Shanequa and a few other kids– all veterans of my goofball homeroom the year before– all tromped back up the stairs to my classroom. Their parents were probably still stuck at work, or trying to make their way home. Someone said they thought the trains were shut down.

Gloria raised her hand. How close to the Twin Towers was 14th street? That's where her mom worked.

I told her it was pretty far, over a mile away at least.

She looked at her hands.

The PA came on- keep whoever you have in your class, the bell schedule is suspended for the rest of the day.

We sat around for the last hour and a half, not doing any real schoolwork. Gloria and Sharron and Shanequa read their books and drew pictures on lined notepaper I handed out; Arthur and Jose sat in the back of the room, talking and occasionally suggested

I should turn on Hot 97 or some other music to make the time go faster.

3:20 PM finally came, and everyone rushed out. It was still sunny outside, you could see the kids bouncing their handballs and basketballs and buying their daily coco gelado from the guy with the handtruck outside, like any other day, just fewer than usual since most of them had been picked up early.

I made my way home, walking from the Bronx to my apartment in Washington Heights. The subways and buses weren't running, and the streets gradually filled with pedestrians walking in the middle of the road. As we crossed the bridge over the Harlem River into Manhattan, several people pointed at the sky, to smoke rising in the distance of Downtown.

11. HAPPINESS

Now it is a strange thing, but things that are good to have and days that are good to spend are soon told about, and not much to listen to; while things that are uncomfortable, palpitating, and even gruesome, may make a good tale, and take a deal of telling anyway.

-J.R.R. Tolkien, The Hobbit

Happiness as a teacher is a matter of habit, and a matter of choice. You get into the habit of doing things that work for you- of checking the homework at the beginning of class instead of bringing a stack of papers home every day, or of keeping the kids' notebooks in the classroom instead of making photocopies of every damn thing- and you realize one day that your last period is over and yet you feel like a civilized human being instead of like Indiana Jones after feeding every snake in the zoo. You also realize that you can choose to berate yourself for every mistake you or the students make, or not. As Bobby McFerrin says, in every life we have some trouble, but when you worry you make it double.

And so most teachers can come across as self-satisfied people, at least in the matter of their work. You can call it a survival strategy- compulsory dissatisfaction day after day will make you start scanning the Help Wanted ads sooner or later- but deciding that what you gave was good enough, even if it was not ideal, is itself probably pedagogically valuable. Just as, for a child, what matters is often less whether their parent yelled at them for the clothes sprawled across the floor than whether they sense their parent is still angry after the yelling is finished, so too the teacher's affect percolates across the classroom and attaches itself to all but the very most socially unaware kid. The same shove between Johnny and Tommy while getting in line for recess can be, depending on the teacher's mood, a momentary hiccup, a Getting In Trouble, or a reason to start hating school. The teacher decides, in the end, whether what is going on in the classroom is acceptable or unacceptable, worthwhile or repulsive, and the kids will generally go along with that judgement, even if they are individually unable to change it.

The teacher- who is powerless in her own classroom in many, many ways, and maybe made still more impotent by administrative mandate and intrusion- retains this single great lever of influence, that she is the organizing principle around which the buzzing, bumbling confusion of one or two or three dozen children or adolescents cohere. This is, no doubt, in part the result of the natural hierarchy of age, and is probably intensified when the children see themselves or who they would like to be reflected in the teacher's mannerisms or diction or gaze. But it is also simply a result of human groups and our desire to organize ourselves around an individual; as Yeats put it:

> They came like swallows and like swallows went,
> And yet a woman's powerful character
> Could keep a Swallow to its first intent;
> And half a dozen in formation there,
> That seemed to whirl upon a compass-point,
> Found certainty upon the dreaming air.

As parent or teacher, as nation or people, we decide whether to be happy; not to accept the unacceptable or not to resolve to improve and to change, but to acknowledge that we are here together and tomorrow will give another chance to try and fail to get it right.

12 THE RAT TEMPLE

I've always been afraid of rats, and when I moved to New York City, I began seeing them everywhere: on the subway tracks of course, but scurrying in tiny teams back into Tompkins Square Park early in the morning (after a night out partying in the Lower East Side), trundling enormously alone into vacant lots in the Bronx, sopoforically stomping on garbage outside my poorly maintained apartment building in Inwood, screeching maniacally in the backyard of the kosher butcher behind our building in Crown Heights. I would see their burrows in the cracks between buildings and in the soil of the community gardens where my middle-school students and I would sometimes go. As everyone knows, in New York City there are a lot of rats.

So when I went to India, I was sure I would see plenty, but I didn't see any. Lots of cows, dogs, pigs, goats, camels, yaks, and monkeys, but no rats. Until I went to the Karni Mata temple.

Karni Mata looks like an ordinary Hindu temple– ornately embossed doors, an entryway where you take off your shoes– and then you pass into the central courtyard and see thousands upon thousands of rats. Screeching at each other in tiny rat voices, patting each other with tiny rat hands, passing in and out of the walls from their secret homes, in constant and impenetrable communication with one another, the rats mostly ignore the visitors who come to gawk at them and share the huge plates of sweetened grains and milk that are left for the rats and which visitors will sample, too. You can pass over a small ornamental bridge to a kind of inner sanctum where a holy man is reading Vedic scriptures out loud, and incense is being burned, and more rats (having passed along the ropes of the ornamental bridge) are eating more grains and drinking more milk.

You have to wonder how they all got there. The story is that they are reincarnated storytellers, in which case this is a substantial portion of all the storytellers that have ever lived, and O. Henry and Mark Twain must be squeakily vying for their section of the milk dish down there, along with Homer and Ra(t)elais.

Certainly it gives the impression of being an isolated population, where the rats not only look alike (who I am I to judge) but have the same weird protrusions from their back end, with an unusually large proportion of albinos (who apparently are especially good luck.) Presumably that isolation is one reason that the visitors to the temple (of which I count myself one, thanks to an unusually persistent and convincing travelling companion when I was in India, despite my fears), don't get sick when they visit or (something I did not do) share food with the rats. There are allegations that the area around the temple was spared an outbreak of plague not so very long ago– were protective antibodies shared with the rats?

Perhaps the temple was there first, and the nest of rats could not be eradicated, and eventually someone started feeding them, and gradually the most even tempered and easily tolerated rats became the ones to predominate. Something like the Soviet scientist Belyaev, who bred wild rats, minks and foxes into domesticated forms (as well as hyper-aggressive forms) over several generations, except largely accidental. The rats I saw in New York, despite their urban environs, are still in most ways wild animals, making their way on their own and fighting it out in a Hobbesian rat world. But the Karni Mata rats, like modern humans, have to worry less about getting enough food and more about going along to get along, not rocking the food-laden boat. The odd-looking, hypersocial, apparently sweet-tempered rats of Karni Mata (at least as long as they get their milk) may be more like domesticated animals, and also more like us.

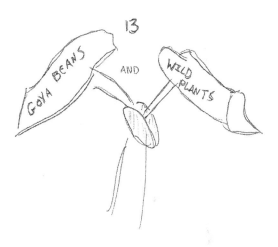

13 GOYA BEANS AND WILD PLANTS

When I left the school in the Bronx, I started teaching 7th grade science in the Lower East Side in Manhattan, teaching Life Science (the middle school version of biology.) I knew I wanted to do more plant labs than I had the previous years. I had taken a Plant Physiology class in college, and the labs were so much more relaxed and pleasant than animal or microbe-based labs. You'd be dissecting cotyledons or whatever, chillin and talking, without the worry of contaminating your bacterial samples, which smelled awful anyways, or the knowledge that you were causing a crayfish great pain.

The 7th grade curriculum was big on experimental design and the effects of varying one variable on an outcome, so I wanted to find seeds that we could grow in great quantities and have the kids come up with questions (ie, what happens when you give it lemon juice rather than water, what happens if you add an extra heat lamp, etcetera.) The first week was a total bust; most of the heirloom seeds I'd bought at considerable cost (120 students adds up) from a hardware store hadn't germinated, and those that had germinated were of so many different species and varieties that it was almost impossible to see how we could do any kind of consistent experiment.

Then I hit upon dried Goya Red Kidney Beans (I tried black beans and dried black-eyed-peas, but the Red Kidneys grew the best.) We put them in several hundred little peat pots on top of the radiator by the classroom window on Friday, and by Monday, the eastern exposure and the overactive radiator had made these guys not only germinate, but push their cotyledons and seed leaves six inches above the soil. The plants were holding up the weight of the clear plastic take-out container tops we'd put over the pots to keep in moisture and produce a greenhouse effect.

Pretty soon, we realized what should have been obvious to me– all of the beans were clones of one another. They sprouted on the same day, flowered on the same day, fruited and formed seed pods on the same day, and looked almost exactly identical except as the vagaries of the classroom environment, their placement in the plant container, and our experimental manipulations altered them. You really could see what more or less light, more or less moisture or heat or lemon juice, did to each of the plants, because they were so much the same to begin with.

*   *   *

A couple of years later, I was camping in Southern Utah when we walked into a field of alpine wildflowers that was growing riotously during the few months of warmth, seemingly dozens of different varieties, all being tended to by squadrons of bees and flies. It would be almost impossible to tell what environmental conditions were doing to any one flower, or even to a section of flowers as a group. After all, the growth course of wild, uncultivated plants is highly variable. Some plants will grow at a rapid rate at first, shooting above the plants around them and grabbing onto sunlight– and then stall out. Others will wait as seedlings for years before shooting up when an opportunity arises. Even within species and varieties, there is enormous variation in growth course and life history between and within populations.

Imagine you went from meadow to meadow, trying to figure out which was the "best" to grow a plant in. The place where the plants were already tallest might be the best– or maybe the plants just got a head start there. So instead you find their initial height and then measure their growth from day to day or month to month, and say that the places where they grew the fastest were the best. Maybe there are some recognizable varieties that are known to grow faster or slower, so you "control" for those differences by giving them a bonus or penalty onto their measured growth rate. You then call the adjusted growth rate the "value added" of the soil and meadow.

Would this make sense? Not really. Even within varieties of a wild plant there is going to be significant variation in the genetically determined life history and growth course. Moreover, the interaction between soil type, water level, temperature, and growth rate will vary significantly from plant to plant, as long as they aren't all the same genetically.

Human intellectual development is much more like the organic growth of wild living things– in fact, it is a form of such growth, of course– than it is like the growth– natural or experimentally modified– of genetically identical Goya Red Kidney Beans.

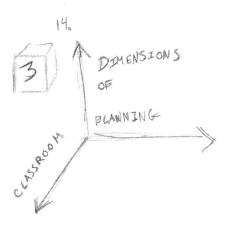

14 THREE DIMENSIONS OF CLASSROOM PLANNING

The average middle or high school class meets around 50 minutes a day, around 180 days a year. That's 150 hours, or 6 and a quarter days. Just in terms of minutes and seconds, it's enough time to, say, see all

36 plays in Shakespeare's First Folio back-to-back, and still have time to listen to the Sonnets at the end, or complete an 18-week plan for preparing for a marathon, twice. It's often forgotten how much of regular-people's jobs are spent preparing for a single presentation or sales talk, delivered multiple times to multiple clients– not a different presentation every day of the year.

Of course, teaching isn't just or primarily about presenting: You're not the sage on the stage, you're the guide on the side, as many a corny professional development coach has advised. A friend and colleague once said- "you're directing a play, but it's a different play every day, and the kids show up not knowing what it is and what their part is going to be." (To which I said, "and sometimes they decide that their part is: throwing paper balls.")

The resolution is repetition of some sort or another. Most of this is repetition of previous classes the kids have taken, and what they think "school" should be: come in, sit down, copy stuff off the board, raise your hand to answer questions, answer practice problems or do classwork worksheets, take tests or write essays, get grades. I don't want to undersell this vision of school. It can seem boring from the outside, and it doesn't conform to what the curricular reformers and professional developers want to see. But success is never boring for kids: if you can make kids feel successful within the context of traditional, formal schooling, and prove to them that they are learning something, that feeling is never boring.

At the same time…look, I'm not saying every class has to be Dead Poets' Society, but there has to be a place for experience, exultation, discovery, shared adventure in school as well as discipline and steady progress. Such opening of experience can go too far. Particularly in science class, it is, as they say in Spinal Tap, such a fine line between stupid and clever. Handing out raw liver for kids to take blood swabs from to look at under the microscope: stupid, at least after Moses swiped a piece to devour on a bet and then projectile vomited on his Special Education teacher later that day. Dipping our heads into a bucket of water to demonstrate the diving response, such that when my principal took a surprise deputation of the Deputy Chancellor and three Assistant Superintendents into my classroom, half the class was chanting "Hold Your Breath, Hold Your Breath" while the other half, heads under water, held out their wrists for pulse measurements, turned out to be clever. (At least it was more clever than it would have been if, when the Deputy Chancellor asked my principal, "is that legal?" he hadn't improvised on the spot and said, "oh…sure, I think it's a very common middle school lab.")

But this is getting very far afield from what this essay was supposed to be about, which is about dimensions of curricular planning: sequence, differentiation, and rigor– or more topographically, longitude, latitude, and altitude. As I said above, the only way to make the incredible *length* of the school year manageable is to employ some degree of structure and repetition. It is with good reason that the one book on every American elementary school teacher's shelf is The First Days of School, which instructs the reader to teach each aspect of the school day, from signing out the bathroom pass to writing a header on notebook paper, as a set of defined and practiced rituals, like "Wax On, Wax Off" only for choosing a new book from the classroom library or picking up missed homework when you were absent.

If there has been a change in American pedagogy in the last couple decades, in fact, it has perhaps been the ascension of the "workshop model" in reading and writing courses, which takes this approach and runs with it: lessons and group activities are compressed into "mini-lessons" (brief expositions at the beginning of the class), and the majority of the class period is given over to individual writing or silent reading, with occasional conferences with a teacher or peer or small group to evaluate or provide feedback. It's a "latitude-first" model: lots of room for individual choice and direction in the day to day and over the course of the classroom period, but relatively little variety in structure or content of the lesson from day to day, as students practice the same reading strategies or writing techniques over and over again. A well-run workshop classroom tends to feel focused, productive, but atomized when you walk into it, with every kid pretty much doing his own thing, marching towards the next Lexile level or assigned compositional form, preparing diligently for the writing prompts and reading passages on the PARCC or Smarter Balanced tests at the end of the year. The workshop model is, for all the idealism with which Lucy Calkins and her army of Teachers' College recruits evangelizes for it, in many ways a realistic resignation to the fundamental challenges facing American teachers– the vast range in ability, particularly in reading, that confronts teachers within an ordinary classroom, along with the diminishing time outside of school that children are likely to spend reading for pleasure if left to do it on their own.

But, in spite of the accuracy of some of the understandings driving the workshop model, you also want to shout– at the army of professional developers, if not at the teachers doing the best they can to accommodate their demands– that the whole rest of their lives will be more than enough time for kids to be alone, independent, working towards individually weighted but collectively immaterial goals. School needs to be about some kind of shared experience and common text, at least part of the time, or it really is almost nothing but the signaling treadmill that Bryan Caplan claims it is.

I have strayed from my task; as Grant Wiggins would put it, the Essential Questions remain unanswered, affixed over the chalkboard but ignored. "Perhaps writing an outline next time would help?" the helpful, imagined, workshop-implementing voice over my elbow inquires of me, no doubt correct. But like the teacher who opens a blank planning book in August to pore over the vast distance from Labor Day to June, or like the reluctant student for whom the single sheet of ruled notebook paper never seems to end, our progress towards goals is often of less importance than how we spend each moment.

15. BUGS

The Giant Malagasy Hissing Cockroaches were a gift
from a student's father, who brought them
unexpectedly and said "keep them warm, and give
them a banana peel now and then." The roaches were
each a little over three inches long, and resembled
nothing so much as a Giant Bug from one of those 50s
horror movies.

Of course, we hadn't just gotten the four or five huge
Malagasy roaches. We got four or five huge
Malagasy roaches, three of which were (in some
bizarre huge-insect way) pregnant. As I didn't until
that moment know, "One interesting aspect of
Madagascar hissing cockroach reproduction is the
females, to some degree, bear live young, as they are

ovoviviparous." Thirty or forty baby roaches escaped from the container (like piglets from a pen), and spread out in all directions just as my 1st period class arrived.

The first kids to come in saw what was coming across the floor and began bolting back into the hallway, where they knocked into other kids trying to get in. They gave up trying to escape and went to stand on their chairs, peering down at the baby roaches running around on the floor and shrieking occasionally.

Some of the roaches were now making for the doors, smelling no doubt the cafeteria three stories below, and ready to turn the day's special of macaroni and cheese into a surprisingly crunchy meal. I could vividly imagine the unflattering picture of myself that would soon appear in the New York Post, underneath the headline—"Roach Food!"

But, as always, among every group, there are those whose bravery emerges unheralded. Luis and Sergey immediately began scooping up the babies into their hands, putting them back into the terrarium, and taping up the sides so they couldn't escape again. Kids began gingerly to step down from their chairs, coming over to watch the mother Malagasy Hissing Cockroaches—so considerate—guiding the babies over to the over-ripe bananas, on which they all chowed down.

In six or seven years of keeping bugs as classroom pets, there were clear patterns of behavior (of the bugs, and the kids reacting to the bugs.)

Giant African Millipedes were sweet-natured and gentle, curling up on your finger like a 700-legged kitten, or drowsily munching on rotten logs for days and days, undisturbed. The kids almost always became quite attached to them, and would become upset if a terrarium was left too dry or mold was found on a vegetable inside. On the other hand, the millipedes were surprisingly good at escaping their terraria in the middle of the night, and the Spanish teacher or the Tech teacher would arrive the next day, red-faced, having been surprised in the teachers' washroom by something crawling across the floor.

Land snails were big hits with everyone, great for races to see which snail could get to the lettuce or the cucumber first. But then they became more heavily regulated, and Carolina Biological stopped selling them.

Crayfish were interesting to everyone, beautiful orange and blue colors and clearly smart and curious as arthropods went, but so foul-smelling when they died that it was better not even to bother.

Wolf spiders would hang out in their cage, unmoving for days, until they jumped on a cricket or ant or whatever we'd give them to eat, just when no one was watching. They will also, if you try to pick them up, bite you quite painfully, even though they can't penetrate the skin, and, much to kids' disappointment, I never became Spiderman as a result.

Mealworms will eat their oats or potatoes until they almost burst, becoming almost unmoving, turn into bizarre HR Giger-like pupae, and emerge as beetles, who will immediately start quite-indecently mating, to the observing kids' horror.

Crickets either die or multiply beyond count. My worst classroom observation was a cricket experiment where they all seemed to have kicked each other dead and even begun to smell rotten in the twenty minutes between setting up the experiment and the principal walking through the door, clipboard in hand.

From time to time, there were other bugs that would arrive, brought by one kid or another-- praying mantises, huge with wicked spikes on their arms, or a piece of bark filled with an ants' nest, or sleeping and hideous cicada grubs. It was assumed that they belonged there, with the rest, and they would be arranged with all the rest of the terraria alongside the window or on bookshelves or next to the fish tanks, for kids to look at when they were bored or when it was time to take a break from learning the parts of the cell or structure and function in the circulatory system.

When we got to learning about cladistics and classification, no one had any trouble believing there were more species of bugs than anything else.

16 BLACKBOARDS WITHOUT A BLANK SLATE

The most obvious thing in the world to educators is how different kids are from one another. Indeed, the beginning-of-the-year faculty meetings in practically any school in the country, even the most racially or economically homogenous, are more likely to focus on these differences than on practically any other aspect of education. "Personalized learning," "differentiated instruction," and "competency-based education" are malleable enough terms to stretch across the vast differences in abilities, interests, and personalities that are supposed to cram into the same classrooms, learn the same curriculum, and (apart from students with IEPs, and sometimes even then) take the same standardized tests.

Over the next few decades, the rapid progress in genetic research will probably make many of these differences among children attributable to genes in clear and unambiguous ways. What then?

Educators are, by their nature and by their choice of profession, committed to the prospect that individual opportunity and effort are the main determinants of success, and almost all teachers, even relatively cynical or pessimistic ones, would be loathe to attribute kids' challenges or failures to genes. In ten years of teaching, I heard a lot from my colleagues about culture, poverty, uninvested parents, poor messages from the media, and self-defeating policies or curriculum. I don't know that I heard genes as an explanation for anything but profound visible disability even once.

But it's possible that will change, that eventually a core of scientific findings will make their way to educators and be accepted. My guess would be that the most likely avenue for this acceptance would be to highlight the possibility of making "genome-based learning" a reality: they'll all learn Algebra II if we just know their As and Ts and Cs and Gs.

But I'm skeptical that such genetic personalization would, in general, lead to much improvement in educational practice or results, and not just because some curriculum may be a poor fit for some kids, regardless of how it is adapted to their learning style, and not just because almost anything dressed up in educational buzzwords is sure to fail.

Frank Smith, the journalist turned psycholinguist, wrote a short but quite profound book called The Book of Learning and Forgetting, where he contrasts what he calls the "classic view of learning" with "the official view." The official view treats learning as work, the classic view says we learn "from the company we keep." The classical view holds that people are constantly and effortlessly learning through immersion in a social community and its practices. The official view suggests that learning only occurs through effort or when a student is being presented with the information.

The fundamental challenge to any attempt at personalization within a classroom, genetically informed or otherwise, is that it makes more difficult the already extremely difficult challenge that all schools face: making the skills the school wants to impart (the readin' and 'ritin and 'rithmetic, along with science and social studies and drivers' ed) part of the school's social community and its practices, the shared body of ritual and collective experiences that determine what kids actually learn.

17 QUALITATIVE AND QUANTITATIVE

1

In your average New York City public middle school classroom, you'll find a fair number of kids who are defiantly opposed to any mention of evolution, especially human evolution. Usually this opposition takes the form of "I don't know about y'all [pointing to classmates], but I didn't come out of a monkey."

There are a number of ways a teacher can address this position. You can emphasize non-human evolution, the safe and less incendiary topics of antibiotic resistance and Galapagos finches, dinosaurs-to-birds and fish-to-salamanders. Hardly any state test will touch human evolution, for fear of scandal, and so you won't be setting them up for failure there (not that anyone cares about science test results anyways.)

Or you can tackle the resistance head on. Take them to the natural history museum's Spitzer (yeah, that one) Hall of Human Origins, and let them gawk and fake vomit at the various model Austrolopithecines and skeletal Turkana Boys, revel in the uncanny valley that makes prehuman hominids seems so very gross, shout at each other "Yo, Arthur, check out your mom," and return happily disgusted and saying with finality, "I still did not come out of that."

My third year teaching I devised what I thought to be a more sneaky approach. Instead of saying we were learning about evolution, we watched one of the early films about Jane Goodall, spent a few days reading one of her shorter children's books, and then went to the Bronx Zoo to watch the gibbons and gorillas in the hooting and grooming and poop-playing flesh. After one kid opined "man, they just like us," or, better yet, "look! the girls are playing with each other's hair and the boys are playing with sticks," then you knew it was time to go onto Darwin.

2

I had another reason for teaching about Jane Goodall, though, beyond remembering her books fondly from when I was myself in middle school, when termite fishing and female estrus behavior both seemed like fascinating things.

The middle school life science curriculum starts with the Scientific Method. There are few topics more frustrating to teach than the Scientific Method.

The They Might Be Giants song "Put It to the Test" says most of what is needed about the importance of experiment, and for the rest you are teaching a structure for telling people about what you have done rather than something that can usefully be followed in anything but the most canned and denatured settings. The kids arrive at middle school jazzed to finally learn some science and suddenly you're talking dumbed-down Popperian falsification.

Jane Goodall may not be the ideal scientist in some respects (in her early years, among other faults, she trained the Gombe chimps to depend on the bananas she supplied rather than their own wild-procured food stuffs), but it is undeniable that she found out new things. The behaviors she observed,not just toolmaking in the form of cleaning twigs to gather termites and chewing leaves to soak up water, but also the details of social hierarchy, group hunting and food sharing, and even making war against opposing communities, were far greater in complexity and variety than what had been observed of captive chimps.

To attempt to measure a behavior is often to eliminate it entirely, an ethological version of Heisenberg's uncertainty principle that I had experienced when trying to study Mockingbird song. Believe it or not, this rule applies in the science classroom as well. Half the time, your 7th grader's well-designed "do the Crickets prefer to hide in plastic egg containers or cardboard ones?"experiment will immediately, as if by magic, lead to half the crickets turning up dead. More importantly, starting with a formal lab protocol and measurement procedure, while teaching useful skills for the next time the kid takes a science class, creates a cognitive hurdle that a good portion of the class cannot o'er-leap.

3

Science starts with seeing, even before measurement, and long before we can start to test a hypothesis in a formal way.

When I left teaching and started studying social science, I kept coming back to Jane Goodall and the chimps. We are but a few steps away from those hairier, stronger primates, as another They Might Be Giants song, "My Brother the Ape," makes clear.

What were the behaviors we didn't see in ourselves, because we were trying to measure them, or because we were measuring the wrong thing? Qualitative social science is a playground for ideology gone wrong, and reliable, representative measurement is probably our only hope at dragging our dreams of infinite human malleability back to earth.

But if we are to see the world as it is- and especially, but not only, the half of us for whom numbers are as slippery and deceitful as a chimp-mashed banana peel left upon the floor- then the first thing to do is to sit before the thing we wish to give up its secrets, be silent, and watch.

18 THE FIRST DAY OF SCHOOL

The greatest thing about being a teacher is that you get to keep doing it. No matter how badly or well a lesson or a schoolday goes, there's another coming after it. So you get another try.

The second greatest thing about being a teacher is that what feels like failure often is, in part or full, a secret success. Often, the best response to kids' having no idea what you were talking about yesterday is to say it again today.

My first feeling of getting through to my crazy 7th grade homeroom my first year teaching occurred when I grabbed a lab out of one of the New York State Standards books, something about using the way different weights of pendulums and the length of the string, affected the period of oscillation, where the kids were supposed to get the idea of varying independent variables to influence a dependent variable.

The lab was a disaster, the washers we were supposed to use as weights for the pendulums flying in back-and-forth projectile volleys across the room. Arthur and Jose, bored with the worksheet on which they were supposed to draw a picture of their experimental design, had set up one barrier with a stack of textbooks on one side of the room, Jeffrey and Danny D set up their own on the other, and reenacted something like the Battle of Austerlitz using handfuls of the small washers. One handful went astray and plinged into the back of Medjine and Sharon's heads, the two girls who had, with iron concentration, completed every stupid lab sheet and every asinine textbook assignment no matter how much riotous nonsense was going on in the back of the room, no matter how sidetracked by writing names on the board or the section sheet and yelling at people to get back into their chairs their incompetent teacher became.

In this case, Medjine brushed the washers out of her hair, stood up, turned around, narrowed her eyes, and quietly said something unprintable to the boys in the back of the room, and then sat back down. Sharron had continued timing the oscillation of the pendulum without stopping.

The bell rang, and the class tumbled out of the room, leaving trampled-on ditto sheets, the strings of floss we were using as the rope to the pendulum, and shiny washers all over the floor.

My usual response to this kind of successful pedagogical experience, for the first several months of the school year, had been to spend an hour or so cleaning up the classroom, head home feeling like I'd been run over by a bus, fall asleep, and wake up in the middle of the night, planning furiously another lesson or lab to make up for the three to six periods of failure that had gone on the day before.

But this time, I just decided the lab had been too complicated, so I cleaned up, made some new dittoes of the same lab handout, and did the exact same lesson again, telling Medjine and Sharron (who rolled their eyes at having to complete the same activity they had done perfectly well the first time) to come up with new independent variables to try.

And so again, and again, until the fourth day there were 32 kids standing silently by their chairs watching the little pieces of floss oscillate back and forth and timing how long it took, and answering pretty coherently when you walked around and asked them what was the independent variable and what was the dependent variable in each of the experiments.

The point isn't that this was great pedagogy, or that they were lucky to be in my 7th grade science class versus any other. It wasn't and they weren't.

No excuses, no regrets, is (my jazz musician uncle once told me) the essential artistic attitude. Being happy in failure, and being happy that what looks like failure is a partial success, and being happy to go home and then blow your horn another day.

At the end of my first year teaching, the night of the last day of school, I went with some friends and fellow teachers down to Coney Island, where we rode the ricketty wooden Cyclone and ran into the water with our clothes on. The first year was done, and nothing could be harder. In my own case, the second year was harder, more dispiriting and humiliating and depressing. But I got to hang on and teach another year, and another, to keep doing it until, by my own lights, what we were doing was really worthwhile.

As the saying goes, parents send their best to school- they're not keeping another, better, set of kids at home. The first day of school has its own awkwardness- the kids and adults sizing each other up, the kids, especially in middle school, wary of each other's potential cruelty and the unpredictability of adult whim. Eventually, though, the classroom becomes familiar if not always comfortable, and for better and worse, everyone's true personality comes out.

In a world of impersonal neighborhoods and virtual work, school is the most important in-person community in many people's lives, for parents as well as kids. I live in the kind of community that Charles Murray described as "Belmont" in Coming Apart- the kind of well-educated and well-employed small town where social norms have in some ways changed little since the 50s (almost all the parents are married, and many of the moms work part time or not at all). If anything, more of our identity has shifted to the kids' lives, and so today, my own kids' first day of school, many of us put the kids on their school bus and then drove over to the school to watch them meet their new teacher for the first time, and then turned around to greet again our more impersonal, less real adult lives, relieved that the summer was over and we could stop worrying about where our kids would spend the day. Life remains stable and pleasant if anxious in Belmont-style America.

The roller-coaster of the school year tugs itself slowly to the top, and then sits for a moment before it will rush downward and forward, like a washer on a piece of string, a pendulum that will swoop back and forth, our oscillations that someone, somewhere, can watch and time and count.

19. WITH THE LAUGHING FACE

My parents' friend B. used to take me out when I was six or seven for hamburgers and tell me about books *like The Daughter of Time* ("why I started liking history," she said) or *Swallows and Amazons* ("better drowned than duffers, if not duffers won't drown," she quoted), or come over to our house and let me help her make a lemon soufflé while explaining Catherine McKinnon-era feminism to me; she moved away but we saw her often afterwards, and she drove with us cross-country the next year when we moved to Los Angeles, during which she taught me the Botticelli guessing game (that I play with my kids at dinner time now) and during which she made a point of stopping for canned shrimp cocktail at every gas station (we joked that one of the cans, all of which looked to have been untouched since the Nixon Administration, was sure to contain botulinum toxin), and during which we made an unsuspecting stop at Molly Murphy's House of Fine Repute in Oklahoma City, where all the waiters were dressed as Prince or Elvis or (in our case) a bunny with a diaper on, and where if you asked for the bathroom all the waiters would come out to scream "Potty Train! Potty Train!" and form a conga line before throwing you into the bathroom.

B. married late, and went through a series of fertility treatments, one of which probably gave her the fast-growing ovarian cancer that killed her in about a year; the last time I saw her, a few months before I graduated high school, she was sick but not diagnosed (they told her it was pneumonia), and we made a soup with twelve heads of garlic and sat in the garlic-smelling house watching a wet Boston snowstorm come down, playing the card game Set and listening to her favorite Coltrane album, Ballads.

The "It Takes A Village To Raise A Child" thing, as employed by politicians, is mostly, of course, an excuse to represent giant and anonymous programs as the natural and unavoidable means of raising children. But the grain of truth is that it should not only be relatives or people whose job it is to take care of us or who have a stake in bringing us up.

Growing up is in large part about finding out what adults are interested in, and learning what it is to be an interesting person. Parents and teachers have to be with us when they don't want to be. They are inevitably, by virtue of overexposure and their role as taskmasters and disciplinarians, uninteresting to us as children more often than not. And so they are often poorly suited to both tasks, of making us interested in the world and of teaching what it is to be interesting ourselves. One of the great losses of our current conception of childhood- which treats, occasionally justifiably, each unrelated adult as a potential mortal threat- is that it makes for fewer people for kids to learn from who aren't there for the sole purpose of being learned from, fewer people who can teach us that adulthood is not just a choice between drudgery and excess. We all need someone to tell us that we are better drowned than duffers, but that if we are not duffers we won't drown.

20. ALL-AMERICAN HIGH SCHOOL

After I left the city and moved to the burbs, I went to teach at the All-American High School. It was All-American because it was wedged between an ultra-rich college town and a perpetually dying small city, and there were mansions and prep schools and boutique farms at one end and dollar stores and free clinics at the other, and in between cul-de-sac after cul-de-sac of 60s split-levels and other regular suburban homes. It was racially diverse but not very socially mixed, except on the sports teams and the cheerleading squad: America.

The school building was mostly brand new (my classroom was in the old hallway, and was ugly and windowless but functional enough) and it was a desirable enough job that the line at the county hiring fair snaked out the door. I told the principal about teaching in the Bronx, about what I thought was important in a classroom, and he was from the Bronx and that was enough to get me another interview, and then another, and another, with different groups of assistant principals or district personnel, until finally I was hired. It was near the beginning of the last recession, when districts were still flush but everyone knew the good times were coming to an end, so they could be choosy. In the end, they hired three new biology teachers, and told us two of us would only have a job for a year, while they transitioned from 10th graders to 9th graders taking the class.

The teachers were, by-and-large, miserable. Not individually, of course: individually plenty of them were able to make the bargain with the students and with the laws of time and gravity that would allow them to spend the period or the year enjoyably enough, and enjoy a good laugh while factoring quadratic equations or talking about *To Kill a Mockingbird* or memorizing the names of cell organelles. But as a group they felt at siege, pulled between parents' demands to get everybody into college, the administration's demands to differentiate every lesson for every kid, and the kids' demands to have a good time and not work too hard.

The principal was a big part of the problem. He was comically out of place: in mafioso dark suit, red shirt, and red tie, he'd drive across the state in an Audi sports car and then spend the day walking the halls and handing out red ballpoint pens embossed with the words "My Principal Believes in Me." All correspondence went through his secretary, and the one e-mail I knew him to have written himself was riddled with spelling and grammatical errors, yet a famous education school gave him a doctorate partway through my first year, proving everything we already knew about education schools. (As my wife remarked, "that guy's a doctor the way Doctor Pepper is a doctor.") He was decent enough at gladhanding with students and patrolling the halls, and he loved to bring groups of popular kids into his office for one "leadership initiative" or another, but he would badger and harangue individual teachers at faculty meetings and in their classrooms in ways that seemed wildly out of control. Once, when a local newspaper printed an article critical of the school that voiced some teachers' concerns, a female teacher in her late 60s, close enough to retirement not to be cowed, stood up in a faculty meeting to say that these concerns were worth discussing as a group. He became almost apoplectic, screaming "You don't know me! You don't know who I am!" while shaking his finger at her, like an audition tape for a Sopranos role.

The Thunderdome nature of my job for the year (three come in, and only one will remain) worried me for a little while, and then stopped. It wasn't that my class was so great- having taught middle school science for so long gave me something to work from, but I was still faking it when it came to high school classes and figuring out what in the giant textbooks was most important and what could be easily forgotten. But I was fairly happy, and so the kids decided to be happy, too. Meanwhile, the other two new teachers ran themselves ragged running after-school sports teams and activities, and got fired at the end of the year for their troubles. It wasn't fair, but what is?

The next year, since they didn't need a biology teacher (half as many students were taking the class), they switched me to teaching the 12th graders who needed an extra credit of science to graduate, along with a new AP class. The 12th graders were sick to death of school, but no longer kids in any meaningful sense, biding their time until they could move to the great beyond of college and become teachers or cops or firemen or doctors like they planned.

It was time for me to move onto my great beyond, too. It might have been the "you don't know me! you don't know who I am!" outburst, which was hardly directed at me (for whatever reason, the Bronx connection among other things meant I was always a favorite of the red shirt/red tie-wearer), but who wants that to be what you look forward to if you stick with the job for another three decades or more? Anyway, it was an excuse to try something new.

The football team was good but not spectacular my two years there: good enough to win the county but then get overmastered in the state tournament, both times. Some of the kids would go on to play in college, but most wouldn't. The one time I went in to see the team an hour or two before a game, to hand over some work that a kid who had been in in-school suspension had missed, it was obvious that the players I knew, goofballs and slackers in science class, were deadly serious, preparing for what they saw as the most important thing in their life, all the more serious because they probably wouldn't be playing again after that year. I've never been much of a fan, but the one Friday night game I saw was similarly riveting, the team solemn and precise in their play and the crowd of parents and fellow students on the edge of their seats.

School is about what school is about.

21 BORED

Boredom is a universal experience of being a student, but managing boredom is a central task of being a teacher, and teaching reveals some aspects of the psychology of the emotion that aren't obvious when you are facing towards the chalkboard instead of away from it.

As a kid, you experience school as a yawning chasm of empty emotional space, sitting at your desk, waiting for something to happen. I spent a good part of second grade, when I couldn't sneak off to the reading corner for an hour or five, trying to figure out how many of a box of pins I found on the floor that I could thread through the skin in my fingers at once without them falling out. ("Twelve.")

So when you become a teacher, one's natural impulse is to try to destroy boredom with variety and unusual activity. Today, we're going to play a board game about multiplying negative and positive integers. Today, you're going to write a poem about the rock cycle. Today, we're going to do this and that and this.

This produces more boredom instead of less. It is not that a variety of experiences are contrary to learning. I am not one to say that dipping your head into a bucket of water or letting huge millipedes crawl over your hand are contrary to the educational project.

But this variety of activity presents a twofold problem. First, kids come to school with the expectation of working towards success, that they will put forth effort, and in return they will be rewarded by not getting into trouble, and a class that is constantly trying one form of instruction and then another gives little in the way of consistent feedback to tell the kid he's doing what he's supposed to do. Second, a class where the teacher is constantly explaining a complex activity tends to require more time listening and less time doing, more cognitive burden just trying to understand what the teacher wants you to do, before it even comes time to try to understand the stuff you are supposed to learn. Together, being stymied in the desire to do some work and waiting, waiting, for the teacher to explain his dumb plan for the day is…boring.

This is particularly true if midway through the teacher's endless explanation there's a fart joke in the back row or a paper ball sailing through the air or someone being poked or a pencil being swiped. You'd think that a class where the teacher is in a failed war against a few troublemakers would be entertaining to the kids not getting in trouble, but instead they often feel oppressive guilt that they did something wrong to make the teacher angry, combined with the unbearable boredom of waiting for the endless conflict to resolve.

The resolution that almost all teachers come to- a strong degree of commonality from day to day to day, a ritualized structure to the lesson, unit, year- is almost the only one available. Within that structure a lot of variation is possible and preferable, and some teachers have such a strong personality that their patter and stories and injunctions and jokes become the continuity that keeps everyone going. But the main tool that experienced teachers have is keeping kids working and feeling marginally successful about it instead of waiting for the adult to announce their lives to them for the day.

As computers take care of more and more of the repetitive and regularized portions of our lives, and as online distractions occupy more of our time, will the remainder of our lives, once we tear ourselves away from those distractions, be varied, unexpected, boredom-free? If teaching taught me anything, it's the opposite: that when we don't know what the day holds, and when we feel little in the way of consistent obligations that matter to other people and that it are in our power to fulfill, we are, more than anything, bored.

22 MODEL, MIRROR, MENTOR

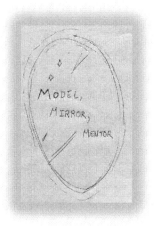

A student contacted me recently who I hadn't heard from in for over a decade. What was he like in middle school, he wanted to know. I told him, in slightly edited detail, about the dung beetle diorama he made, the poster excoriating the school in rude words and angry pictures that he held up one day in the hallway while going from class to class.

A friend of mine calls conversations like this the "mirror role" of being a teacher, telling students how they seem to the world, in slightly edited detail. There are other roles, the mentor role, which is what people seem to think test scores can measure, and the model role, where students use you to figure out who they want to be or not to be, now or in the future.

I should say that the existence of any of these roles, or the psychological importance that a kid places on one adult or another in his life is in no way in contradiction to the proposition that the net impact of any given teacher or adult is, in general, approximately zero. If this kid hadn't found you to mentor him or to reflect back what he is or could be, to show one possibility of what he could become, he would have found someone nearly as good or better, at least in our mostly wealthy, mostly forgiving society.

Does that mean that all teachers are equally good? Of course not, and it especially does not mean that all teachers are equally good for every kid. That we could have found, in one model or mirror or mentor's absence, another to serve the same role does not mean that the role itself made no difference, or could not have been played poorly or well.

To measure anything is in some way to corrupt or distort that thing, the Heisenberg uncertainty principle of social behavior as of electron orbitals and shells. That doesn't mean that even flawed measurements are entirely content-free. When the New York Times in 2010 irresponsibly released the VAM (value-added model) scores of every third through eighth grade math and reading teacher in the city, was I shocked by any of my former colleagues' or friends' scores? No, of course not. Is VAM mere chicanery, no more scientific than 16th century alchemy? Probably, though those alchemists had some insights into practical chemistry that came in handy later on.

If we find that on average, controlling for genetic confounds, a parent makes little or no difference in how their kid ultimately turns out, is it necessarily true that teachers make none too? Perhaps, perhaps not. My own sense is that you can teach your own child a single thing, that they not you are the main determinant of, and for the rest you're just making memories together, filling the time from breath to breath.

When I was ten or eleven I found two mirrors in the back of a closet and arranged them looking at each other, hoping to glimpse infinity. But, as in social science, in the center of the concentric reflections of mirrors I saw only enveloping darkness, along with my own irritating and intruding eye.

23 BOYS VERSUS GIRLS

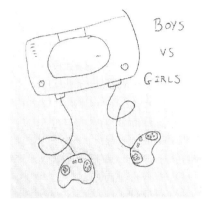

My last few years teaching middle school, I did morning yard duty- watching the schoolyard in the twenty minutes before kids were let in to go up to homeroom. Every day, 30 to 35 boys would show up at the schoolyard as early as they could get there. It was a different game every day, basketball or football or dodgeball or "Booties Up"—an invented game, kind of like handball, but with more aggressive penalties. With the exception of basketball, which naturally divides itself between the proficient and the novice, there were few social distinctions in these games. The dorks ran after the dodgeball just as avidly as the superstars, joyfully cursing at each other and screaming for the ball. Boys at their best—self-motivated, self-organized, inventive, ready to (loudly and with many curses) peacefully resolve their disputes.

And then we would go upstairs to class.

Middle school is a time of great division between boys and girls. And one thing that middle school girls, for the most part, do, and boys, for the most part, do not, is get good grades and do well in school.

But why do girls do better? My experience has been that, at least in middle school, girls are just as likely to get into serious trouble– fights or arrests or drugs or running away—as boys. (At my first school in the Bronx, I mentally nicknamed one wild group of girls the Maenads, after the dangerous devotees of Dionysus in Euripides's play.) And yet girls, on average, get much, much better grades than boys, on average.

This is because girls, on average, do more homework, more classwork, and do better on most in-class tests, than boys. The boys I taught middle school might launch matchlessly into class discussions of subcellular functions or Darwinian evolution, but they couldn't remember a pencil, couldn't remember a notebook, couldn't remember their homework, couldn't remember to stay in their seats. Maybe it was ever thus. I couldn't remember my own homework or pencil or notebook or where I put my lunch; I'm sure Tom Sawyer was the same way; and I'm sure Euripides had to borrow a pencil from the Maenad in the next row.

Maybe it's our biological heritage, a dysfunction in our Y chromosomes that makes turning in homework on time impossible. I think of a scene from Jane Goodall's work with the chimpanzees of Gombe: a mother chimp sits at a termite mound, patiently fishing a twig in and out to catch termites, her young daughter just as patiently imitating her technique. Meanwhile, behind them, the chimpanzee's son swings around a big branch and snorts.   I showed the movie to my class and everyone laughed in instant recognition. There it was, the girls paying attention in class and the boys playing with sticks.

Is it that boys' heads are too full—of video game cheat codes, horror movie plotlines, rap lyrics and NCAA scores—for them to remember the mundane ingredients of school success? All around them, the bustling buzzing confusions of our culture swirls, for them more impossible to ignore than the Maenad in the next row. Get a bunch of twelve-year-old boys in a room together, and they'll launch into minute metaphysical examinations of video games and Saturn's moons and the election and the hybrid car engine.   But the realism required by school eludes them.   It wasn't that all my students in the Bronx or elsewhere wanted to be rappers or ball players. It was that a good number of the rest wanted to be Spiderman.

24 Happy Holidays

It's a funny thing, but the onset of winter in a New York City public school is mostly an experience of heat, the steam radiators clanking louder and louder as they are pushed up to twice full blast. Soon, every window on one side of the building is open, with convection currents visible as the Board of Ed's capital budget vanishes into the chill December air. So much for efficiency.

Even with the windows open, it's a dry, toasty, feeling in those classrooms in the winter, as you move about the room with your gradebook open, half the kids still in their parkas, complaining about the draft, and half lolling off their chairs in damp oversized t-shirts, funky with sweat. "Open up your homework open up your homework open up your homework," you ratatatat repeat yourself, and walk by with a stamp or a checkmark and a swift (and possibly meaningless) mark in the gradebook, because who the hell can collect 200 homework assignments every day to grade: as the stacks and stacks of papers on your desk attest, "not you."

For yourself, your continuous motion, unnecessary and pointless though it is, and ratatat speech- "I see Eric has his paper out and is copying the lesson 'AIM,' I see Vanessa already put her homework out on her desk," keeps you flushed and parched, on both the good days and especially on the bad. After a hyperkinetic late November double period with class 7-211, in which Heriberto stepped up onto his chair and then jumped from one desk, to another to another, and then- shouting "Matrix!"- vaulted onto the front lab bench, in evident imitation of Keanu Reeves, knocking a large Erlenmeyer flask into the nonfunctional sink with a crash, you find yourself unable to hear out of one ear, and convince yourself that 7-211 has delivered to you an early life stroke, but it turns out just to be dehydration, nothing that half of a gallon jug of water from the bodega can't cure.

This is how Jerry C. finds you, sprawled like a drunkard half out of your spinny chair, the gallon jug loosely dangling from one hand, when he appears, tiptoeing into the room grasping a bathroom pass from art class, and explains that you can't keep sending Heriberto to the dean's office when he does things like jumping onto tables, because while Heriberto is 16 in the seventh grade and Heriberto's girlfriend is 20 and in college, she has promised to "divorce" him if he is still in seventh grade when she turns 21, which will happen if you keep sending him out of class. You restrain yourself from remarking on how Heriberto's girlfriend, while no doubt a wise woman, might be better served by pushing the logic of this ultimatum just a bit further, and stop yourself from confiding in Jerry how Heriberto's skills in romance evidently far outpace your own, your own nighttime activities presently consisting of staring balefully at the stack of 200 papers sitting on your desk at home and trying to dream up ways of keeping everyone from jumping on the desks. You let Jerry know you will bear Heriberto's marital obligations in mind and beseech Young Cupid to hie himself back to art class, faster than arrow from his own bow, and after the classroom door closes behind him you take another swig from the gallon jug and sigh.

But that was weeks ago, and now the winter holiday appears in all your minds, your and the kids' both, like a psychedelic snowflake in an old TV Christmas special, spinning and entrancing you all with its limitless possibilities. It seems that while there were moments of excitement earlier in the year (the week of the Subway World Series comes to mind, when most of the 7th grade boys stumbled into homeroom each morning like exhausted gamblers after a long night at the tables) there were few moments of hope the way these weeks feel themselves to be, suffused with the promise of freedom from one another and a little peace and quiet, which, no doubt, they crave as much as you. At any rate, your pedagogy has made one small bit of progress; an incipient bronchitis means you can no longer yell, and so your constant refrain of "who has their books out? who is ready to get started?" comes in more of an affectionate croak than the bullying bellow that had been your habit earlier in the year. The students occasionally look up, an expression of pity on their faces ("dear lord, what have we done to this man?") and get out their papers and copy whatever nonsense is on the board, out of compassion more than anything else.

The day before the break, they cannot stop smiling, and stride into each period to surround you, demanding whether there will be a Christmas party with soda and treats, the way their elementary teachers would do.

"Yeah, my man," Heriberto reaches over the little kids surrounding you, to pat you on the shoulder, in an older-brotherly kind of way. "We can have a party, we can teach you to bachata and merengue, so you can have some fun. You need to lighten up, you know that?" And he goes and sits on top his desk, with his notebook open on his lap, ready to Do Some Work.

You don't have soda or cake, but you printed up some of the stupid science vocabulary crossword puzzles they love to do as long as it doesn't require any thinking, as long as they have all the words along the side and are just matching letters and boxes and don't really have to figure out what any of the words mean, and while they eagerly work on this important task, you walk around the alternately hot and drafty room, and pass out to each of them individual sheets from a Far Side daily calendar that you had torn out and written on the back, "Dear Julio [or Delores, or Nayales or so on], I hope you have a wonderful holiday and a Happy New Year," to each of them.

A gift, in its small and paltry way, and most of them recognize it as such, and take it with them rather than leaving it with the half-done crossword puzzles on their desks, when they leave for their two weeks of freedom, and you find left on your desk, next to the untouched and dusty stack of papers, more substantial gifts, most Christmas-related, ceramic Nativity scenes and a large electric clock with angels and baby Jesus, a matched shirt-and-tie set and a CD of mixed merengue and bachata songs.

25 THE TALENT SHOW

From my 3rd through my 5th years teaching middle school, when I had left the school in the Bronx and was working in the Lower East Side, another teacher and I ran a school talent show, first once a year and then twice. There was a comedy act or two, a rock band, a chorus elective led by the two school secretaries and singing Motown songs mostly, some student films made under the auspices of a filmmaking elective the two of us taught, some teacher skits and joke music videos, one of which you can still find on YouTube, some gymnastics routines, a few socially inept boys playing piano, lots of girls singing pop songs, a rapper or two, one or two Chinese-language and Spanish-language singing acts, and lots and lots of dance acts, some good, some terrible. When I started at the school- also when I started helping out with the talent show- the school was a tiny set of five classrooms on one end of the third floor hallway that was mostly given over to administrative offices for the city's school safety officers, above two small but not as-small elementary schools on the two floors below, and for a month or two before the talent show the little microcosm of a school would get consumed by auditions, rehearsals, film production, gathering the sound equipment and piecing together backup bands for the chorus, tearful fights among dance groups with creative differences, begged entreaties for this kid or that to join somebody's act, flyers and posters promoting the various acts of the show, along with the secret preparations for whatever silliness the teachers had planned, which usually involved "leaked footage" of teachers sneaking out of detention or of the principal wearing a do-rag and gold chains; you get the idea. Teaching middle school is full of agonies and disappointments but in one way it is far superior to teaching high school: the kids are still at an age in which the school is their world, and most of us teachers were young enough in spirit or reality to have little in the way of competing demands on our time and emotional energies.

The following year I got married and my first child was born; midway through the school year our district superintendent was visiting and, always presumptuous, buttonholed me at the door of my classroom to ask me why I wasn't running the talent show anymore. I explained that family life was keeping me pretty busy, to which she replied, "well, the baby isn't here *yet!*" True enough, although giving up the show, along with simply spending fewer evenings in the school building, had probably made me a better teacher and made my science class finally closer to what I was going for all along; giving half of yourself to a community and keeping some in reserve is often more efficacious than giving all. But occasionally, even now, I'll hear one of the mid-2000s pop songs that were the talent show's bread-and-butter and find myself nodding and tapping along. I wonder if the reason so often we find our musical tastes fixed in our late teens is not merely because of our declining neural plasticity but because we never again have the experience of being in the madding crowd the way we were in school, among those who would teach us to love a new or new-to-us song; surely the formation of our tastes is a matter of who we would think ourselves like or akin to as much as it is a dispassionate judgment of aesthetic form.

The talent shows themselves were seemingly epic in the moment, even if in reality they only stretched from six-thirty to eight or so: fifteen to twenty five acts going on one after another, with a crew of hyperalert miniature roadies passing up and down microphones and instruments on and off the stage and eyeing the set list gravely to see what was coming next, and the audience of students and parents and eventually alumni of the school waving their cell phones back and forth in imitation of lighters at a concert, and at least sixteen different boys standing up and pretending to hold the winning raffle ticket when the PTO president got up midway through the evening's entertainments to demand silence and announce the results of the fundraiser they had held at the door. Then the principal would stand up and shush the boys and ask for silence for the next act, for the tiny kid waiting anxiously in suit-and-tie to go play piano or the six girls dressed in marginally-school-appropriate outfits on the wings of the stage to go dance to "Hot in Herre" or "Pan de Replay," and the boys holding up the imaginary raffle tickets would snicker at the principal and then sit down, knowing that in another three acts the teacher skit would start and the principal would be revealed onstage in do-rag and basketball jersey, demanding candy over the PA system or throwing paper airplanes in the faculty meeting. This was the agreement we made in that school for its first few years- that we'd do our part to make the school a fun-enough place and the kids would work reasonably hard and treat us like human beings when they could, and forgive us the disorganization and mishaps of trying something new.

The talent show didn't make anybody learn much more, of course, or learn more at all, but the point of school is hardly learning, but to figure out a way to be in the same building with a bunch of other people day after day after day, to clap when the lights come on and laugh even when a joke doesn't quite go right, to do your piece and then let somebody else go onstage and do theirs.

26 Colleagues and Friends

I had been hired at my first school in late August, about ten days before the beginning of school. The hiring for the district in the Southwest Bronx was happening in a single room in the district office, a small storefront under the elevated 4 train where the walls would shake periodically as a train went by overhead. My TFA project director, a round-faced, California hippy with short-clipped blond hair (she would later tell me she got through her first year teaching with the help of a lot of high-quality chronic bud) guided me over to a set of four desks pushed together, where two overweight men were seated in too-small desks: a white guy in his early 60s with a steel-gray beard and cold, detached blue eyes, sweating profusely in a shirt-and-tie with the sleeves rolled up, and a younger black guy with long dreads in a dark suit. The white guy introduced himself as Forman, the black guy as Trimmingham, and the white guy started in on a speech he had clearly made several times already that day.

"We're reorganizing the school into professional learning communities where the students will be guided into curricula that are targeted to their individual interests and project based learning opportunities for exploration matched to areas in the arts and future careers these small learning communities will allow for a smaller and more intimate school within a school experience" he said, without audible punctuation. He switched off the robotic patter, and said, in a more normal tone of voice, "I've been in the school system for thirty five years, and I've been an administrator for twenty years." He paused, as if he expected me to say something.

"Has it changed a lot in that time?" I said.

Trimmingham, the black guy, laughed. "Thirty five years, I'd think it's changed a lot."

Forman, the white guy, half-smiled. "There's…more attention on the schools than there used to be, from the public and from parents. Which is good, even if it makes things harder sometimes. But the kids are the same as they ever were." And he looked at me meaningfully, as if he expected me to protest that the kids were much different thirty five years ago. He looked down at my resume. "You've worked in schools before?"

I explained what I'd been doing in Philly, the good parts at least. Forman looked at Trimmingham and shrugged in a, "sounds good enough" type of way. It was summer 2000, unemployment was the lowest it's ever been in New York. I was good enough.

"What would I be teaching," I asked.

"Earth science…or physical and life science. 6th grade and 7th grade, or 7th and 8th grade, or maybe all three. We'll have the assignments in the next two weeks." (School started in less than two weeks.) "Five classes, or six. You'd be the main science teacher for one of the new academies."

I said yes, since I assumed that's what I was supposed to do when somebody offered me a job, and they both shook my hand, Forman's handshake bone-crushing and Trimmingham's huge hand soft, barely clasping mine.

"You feel good about this?" my TFA project director asked me, as I walked away from the cluster of desks. I shrugged, in a "sounds good enough," type of way. "You'll be fine," she said, with a wide smile, her short blond hair bobbing.

Then it was down the hall, to get fingerprinted and get assigned an emergency teaching credential. The guy reading through our college transcripts to see if we had enough science credits to teach science stopped and shook his head as he scanned mine.

"You need at least four credits of physics," he said.

I pointed to my freshman year grades.

"Auto mechanics doesn't count as physics," he said.

I explained that mechanics was a pretty hard introductory physics class at my school, and agreed with him that they should fix the name since it was confusing. He handed me a slip of paper that said that I could teach as a permanent substitute for the year but would need six credits of instructional methods courses if I wanted to keep my credential at the end of the year. I was a teacher, more or less.

I took the subway down to the 63rd street YMCA, where TFA was putting us up while we got jobs and found apartments. My roommate had just gotten back from an interview elsewhere in the Bronx.

"I got a job."

"Me, too. 6th grade math and science. Or 6th and 7th grade math. They don't know."

"Yeah, me, too. A bunch of classes, they don't know which ones."

It was still early afternoon: a dull, hot August New York day. I decided to go look for an apartment, and took the A train up to 181st street, and walked into the first real estate office I saw.

An Italian guy with a round, clean-shaven face introduced himself as Louie, how much was I looking to spend.

"I got a place that's just perfect. It's 550 and the heat's electric so your electric bill's gonna be crazy, but it's 550 for your own apartment. Penthouse- well at least it's on the top floor."

The apartment, a tiny studio with a strange plasticky smell from the thick layer of sealant covering the floor, was on the seventh floor, but because it was below Fort Tryon's huge hill, it was actually below the bottom floor of the apartment building behind it.

"Yeah, sure," I said.

The next day was Saturday. I spent a while going from bookstore to bookstore, looking for middle school science textbooks, trying to figure out what I'd be teaching the following year. Then the rest of the New York TFAers were meeting at the apartment of the TFA board president, a telecom executive, and her famous nonfiction writer husband.

This was a real penthouse, looking out at the sun setting over the Hudson from the West Side, and waiters in cummerbunds circulated, offering us shrimp and little mushroom hors d'oeuvres speared on toothpicks. I saw my round-faced, blond program director.

"This is making me a bit nervous, like you guys wouldn't be wining and dining us like this if this weren't a big mistake, " I said.

She smiled. "Not a mistake, just hard."

The famous nonfiction writer husband was holding forth to a group of four or five male corps members.

"You gotta ask yourself, is this something I love? I mean, I was a lawyer, and I hated being a lawyer. But hell, when I became a parent, I didn't know any seven year olds."

The telecom exec gathered everybody together in the center of the enormous living room, said a few words about how proud of our (not-yet-begun) service she and the famous nonfiction writer husband were, and, probably eager to get rid of us, had the waiters hand out tickets to the Circle Line cruise that night.

One of the other guys had a bottle of wine but no corkscrew. We managed to cork the bottle and pass it around to take a swig while looking at the lights of the city, as the boat circled around the island.

27 Don't Be Fooled by the Rocks That I Got

In a few dreams I've had as an adult, I appear in my current age, time traveled back to a few years or months before I was born. I hang out, on a sunny day next to my grandparents' pool, a friend of somebody nobody can quite put their finger on, making jokes with my uncle or making funny faces at my older brother, still a baby in the dream. These dreams are the exact reverse of the ones you have of being a student (or, in my case, often of being a teacher): instead of arriving midway through the semester with months of work to catch up, delinquent and delayed, impossible to make up the time you have lost, the classroom a dreary mess, the desks out of order and the kids surly and suspicious and the teachers exasperated at your long absence, the dreams of the time before you are born have a wonderful sense of peace and security and lightness- there is no time to make up, no expectations to have failed- you don't yet exist, are just an idea or not even that, and can't possibly disappoint; perhaps this is why when I talk to my grandparents in these dreams, their not yet middle aged faces kind and happy, they never demand to know who I am or why I have come there- they are pleased to have me relax, outside of time, in the sunny afternoon of the before-time. Even my parents, holding forth in the self-assured and voluble way of young people, in the corner of my mind's eye, are best left to their own devices, as I know that I will be trouble enough for them soon enough.

The great treasure of the world, the great joy, is that of possibility- not our own, but the one we are given and pass on to another, the sunny afternoon that glitters and does not fade.

One of the more sensible people that Teach for America had speak to us when we were getting our 5-week training was a former TFA teacher who had gone back to school and become a family counselor. She said that most parents could worry less about whether they were good or bad parents, but whether they were "good enough"- whether they passed a fairly low and forgiving bar from day to day. Similarly, despite Teach for America pushing the idea of the outstanding teacher as a transformative force in poor children's lives, on an average day it probably made more sense to think less about being an awe-inspiring superstar and more about being a "good enough" teacher- passing your own forgiving bar, by your own standards, as best as you can.

It's a concept that I think we could do with applying more broadly. American schools could arguably be improved further, but it is to me quite hard to argue they don't pass some low bar of adequacy; in all but the most chaotic schools, motivated children on average do well, even if not as well as they conceivably would in the best of all possible settings.

The simple fact is that there is no one way to improve our schools, nor are the needs of school systems any more universal than the needs of the five and six and seventeen year olds entering them each year. We are a wealthy nation,- where most kids in the public school system are designated as poor, eligible at least for free or reduced price lunch, a still-predominantly white country where most public school students are not white. And we are a nation that has, at least over the last several decades, viewed its schools as an almost continuous crisis and concentration of failure, even as pouring in far more expenditure per student than any comparable country.

The solutions proposed for this continuous crisis are well-known, even if they are allocated to different political voices at different times. Conservatives have argued for choice and competition, for charter schools and vouchers for private schools and easier homeschooling, as well as kneecapping the power of teachers' unions and the ability of districts to expand their budgets at will. Liberals have argued not just for more funding and smaller class sizes but for conscious programs of socioeconomic integration and racial desegregation. Technocrats have argued for more precisely measured indices of teacher and school performance, and serious-minded centrists have argued for higher academic standards and more challenging tests. A million different providers of curricula and interventions (perhaps literally) have argued for their particular programs and methods as the singular agent of change that will transform the schools.

It is likely that as the nation's schools become more obviously poorer than the nation as a whole that the sense of crisis that has been our shared narrative will be more and more appealing, to all participants in the political system. Education is purported to be the "civil-rights issue of this century," as some of my friends and former colleagues from Teach for

America are fond of saying, and though I think this is confused as to the nature of rights and the capacities of the state, I also know that to be a teacher is to experience yourself as the guardian and shepherd of that Beloved Community of which Martin Luther King spoke, among the small desks and small people, in your little domain between the pencil sharpener and the air conditioner. The truth is that the aspirations of shared purpose and common quest is what keeps schools and classrooms, those societies in miniature, functioning to the extent they do, and I cannot in good faith resent the tendency for educators in particular to apply that same vocabulary to the nation as a whole, even if I believe it to be misplaced.

A few years ago, the governing idea about urban education, if you picked up a magazine or newspaper, was that the reason that school I taught at in the Bronx was screwed up was because the teachers were all lazy or stupid, reading the newspaper instead of teaching. But the veteran teachers I knew well all worked hard, all tried to understand the kids on their own terms as well as to communicate Rikki-Tiki-Tavi and the Revolutionary War and math proportion problems in the kids' terms, as best as they could, and to communicate what it was to be a reasonable, thoughtful adult as best they could as well. There were times they no doubt felt themselves to be in a war against the kids who ran through the halls, peeking into a quiet, studious classroom to yell out "Wassup, Wesssssst-Side!" and then running away, and times my colleagues, like me, took things too personally with this kid or that. But mostly, they did their best, and it was hard to see that substituting another person in the room instead of them, someone younger or more expensively educated, would make an appreciable or positive difference on average. Putting me in there certainly wasn't changing the world.

American education is a frustrating, imperfect thing, not only in its execution but in its nature, and the scope of schools to solve the problems of American society is limited at best. Even the most successful possible incarnation of American schooling will not look like "success," even if many parents and kids and teachers will feel successful, nor will it, most likely, produce especially impressive test scores by international standards. It will look- and will be- unjust and unfair as well as unequal. There is the occasional Platonic philosopher king in the American school system, but she is busy teaching first grade.

Much of adulthood is learning to live with diminishing returns. Our best efforts, at work or love or the rest of life, are often less productive than our half efforts. As with the pint of ice cream hiding in the freezer, devouring some is usually better than devouring all.

But we have a harder time applying that insight to public policy. Our society can help some people some of the time with some expenditure of resources. But whether we can help more people more of the time with greater expenditure of resources is not simply a matter of being "smart" in our interventions, of listening to the results of "evidence-based policy."

Human beings are resilient things, that to themselves are often true, even when those selves are not how we want them to be. Parenthood generally involves this recognition, that our dreams for other people must ultimately bow before the person they are bound to become.

But when it comes to other people's children we have a harder time managing this acceptance. We acknowledge that college seems to be the sole ticket to a comfortable middle-class life, so we design ninth grade curricula and six grade curricula and third grade standardized tests that presuppose everyone taking them is on the train to an academic degree, at a "good" 4-year school.

Recognizing that this is not in fact the case, that many and probably most children in the country are not going to complete an academic degree, does not mean counting those children out of the society, or presuming before we could possibly know that their future is predetermined to be X instead of Y.

It is not that we are free of obligation to other people's children, if only because they will determine the character of the society when they grow up. But those obligations are to the place they grow up in- that it is clean, and safe, and well-lit, and has enough kind people to talk with and books to read and space to play in, enough air and color and life. No doubt many schools do not fulfill this minimal list.

The commitment of the society, that can still be largely fulfilled, is to provide an adequate place for kids to grow up in. But it is they who are doing the growing up.

Heraclitus, the pre-Socratic philosopher, is said to have said:

"Everything changes and nothing remains still … and … you cannot step twice into the same stream…We both step and do not step in the same rivers. We are and are not."

The adult who steps across a stream may be a different person when he returns a year later, but a three-year-old, or a seven-year-old will be a really different person a year later. Adults may be ever-changing, but children are really ever-changing, in ways moderated not just by their environment and who they were yesterday, but by the invisible counterpoint of the unfolding changing world and the child's genes.

Practically every teacher who sticks with it for a while has had the experience of a former student returning to them years later to tell them, "man, your class saved my life," to which you as teacher ask yourself, "really? All I remember is you and Jason playing paper ball soccer with each other on the desk." But to that kid, at that time, it made a difference. Perhaps any half-way competent teacher would have made the same difference; perhaps if it hadn't been you it would have been someone else the following year.

All the kid knows is that he has returned to the river, and neither he nor the river is the same.

The crazy school I taught at in the Bronx also had a lot of smart, studious kids, who were, in a way, extra-smart and extra-studious because of all the bozos acting up around them. I'll never forget Carlos raising his hand the first day of school to explain why he wanted to be a chemist, or Jose, only a few months after arriving in the country, working through a persuasive essay explaining the evidence for continental drift, or Sharron's raised hand and precisely-worded answers, day after dreary day, as the rest of her goofball class hooted and hollered and laughed and tossed paper balls. And I'll never forget the days that this kid or that decided it was time to get their act together, Eric staying after school day after day to finish the stupid worksheets I gave as homework, eager for me to call his mom and tell her how good he was doing, or the soda-bottle water rocket that Danny J. made after school in the classroom, carefully cutting out the wooden fins and painting it all silver, that he and I then launched with a bicycle pump in the middle of recess, the silver rocket plopping up four or five feet before it splashed down in a fountain of bubbly water, the other kids who had assembled in an enormous circle around the rocket falling over with laughter, crying with mirth.

It was, in a way, easy for a kid in that school to decide that it was time to make something of him or herself, in part because once you did, no one could mistake you for the kids wandering into school at noon without a bookbag or getting hauled off to Juvie in the middle of the year. The serious kids at that school were, in a way, more serious than the serious students when I taught in more affluent schools later on, since their identity was such a clear contrast to the near-chaos all around. Do I think they held onto that identity for good, once they made it out of middle school? It's unlikely; once they made out of that ugly mass of cinderblock in the Southwest Bronx, it was going to be harder for them to stand out from the crowd. I've kept in touch with one or two, and they are genial and well-mannered adults now, holding onto their Bronx identity with wry amusement as they've moved and changed. As Jennifer Lopez, who grew up a few blocks from the school I taught at, sang:

Don't be fooled by the rocks that I got

I'm still, I'm still Jenny from the block

Used to have a little, now I have a lot

No matter where I go, I know where I came from (South-Side Bronx!)

Feeling different from where we're from, and longing for it once we've left, are the modern condition, and even if we stay on the block where we're from, it will change and leave us behind. My second year teaching, the veterans of my crazy homeroom the year before, now aged and venerable 8th graders, would sometimes speak of 7-221 with nostalgia and a note of pride, ("we were the best!" they'd say to me, contrary to all evidence) for even the worst pieces of our lives are precious to us if they are ours.

28. THE RAINFOREST AND THE SALT MARSH

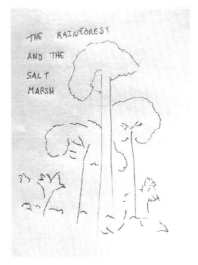

Rainforests are arranged in horizontal layers, and many animals spend their whole lives in a single layer, never venturing up from the forest floor or down from the canopy, for example. The ultimate source of energy for the whole system is the same (sunlight), and everything is in the end competing for sunlight, or to eat the things that captured the sunlight, or to eat the things that ate the things that ate the sunlight, or just to eat wastes and decayed remains of one kind or another. But while the source of energy is all the same, the physical structure of the system, combined with its year-round warmth and year-round rainfall, allows for a near-infinity of niches for organisms to inhabit (particularly small organisms like beetles), with the result of the famously huge number of species in a single rainforest.

Surprisingly enough, while tropical rainforests have very high primary productivity, the amount of sunlight energy trapped through photosynthesis and made into living things or used for living, they aren't uniquely high. Salt marshes, for example, the endless ugly wet stands of partially submerged grass near the mouths of rivers into the ocean (you see them near East Coast airports very often), beloved by biting bugs and birdwatchers and not many else, have essentially the same primary productivity as tropical rainforests.

Salt marshes, despite being very good at capturing sunlight and turning it into living stuff, tend to have quite low species diversity. The reason, as I understand it, is that the estuaries and brackish water present a problem that only a small number of organisms can solve– surviving in a wide range of temperatures, moisture levels, and especially salinities. Often salt marshes attract a wider diversity of migratory birds, but like the old joke about Hell, things look different when you're a tourist. For organisms stuck there year round, the number of different obstacles and constraints that the salt marsh imposes mean that the number of potential biological solutions is much smaller, yielding lower species diversity. A stand of marsh grass benefits from the harsh conditions of its sometimes salty, sometimes freshwater, sometimes warm, sometimes freezing, sometimes dry and often inundated environment; it can solve the problem that few other organisms can solve, and it benefits from the lack of competition. Moreover, the physical homogeneity of the environment leaves few niches for organisms to inhabit- it's all just one big mess of muck, without the individual microhabitats that distinguish the rainforest.

When we think about the forces that would contribute to intellectual or cultural pluralism versus monotony, we might think about both the rainforest and the salt marsh. The salt marsh makes everyone play by the same rules, and they are a very challenging set of rules, with multiple competing simultaneous problems to solve. The result is that only a small set of solutions can survive- the same sea grasses and same few species of animals over and over again. The rainforest both allows more independent subenvironments to persist, and allows each of those subenvironments to impose its own rules on its inhabitants. An organism struggling for survival in each of those niches does not experience its life as easy or forgiving– nature is red in tooth and claw in the Amazon every bit or more as in the marshlands– but the threats that nature imposes are more local, specific, and varied from place to place, with the result that far more varied solutions can result.

We should think about if we are making our schools a forest or a marsh.

13 WAYS OF GOING ON A FIELD TRIP

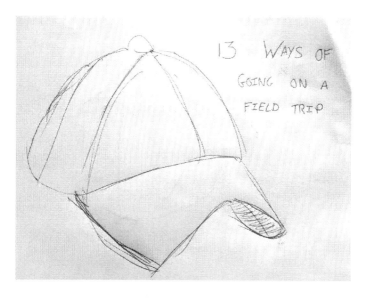

1.   (by plane)

When I was working for the community service program in Philly, before I started teaching, I went as a chaperone with a group of high school kids I'd never met, to Alex Haley's "farm" in Tennessee (really more of a training center) as part of a summer program the School District of Philadelphia was organizing with the Children's Defense Fund, where high school kids would be trained to act as tutors for elementary kids for summer school. The kids had obviously been chosen to be the kind of poor 16-year-olds you could take on a plane and have stay in a hotel without havoc breaking loose; only a few of the kids were a bit more adventurous, and me and the other chaperone camped out in the hall and turned back a few boys making a run for the girls' rooms in the middle of the night; there was also one graffiti incident (I think it was Marian Wright Edelman yelling at us about it the next morning and telling us how disappointed she was, but I'm not sure).

What was more interesting was the design of the two day training itself, which had zero to do with how you help a seven year old learn to read, but had a mesmeric focus on the Civil Rights movement (the theme was that the high-schoolers were going to be running "Freedom Schools" through their tutoring, analogous to the 1964 Freedom Summer), and an insistence on Afrocentric elements (there was a Swahili call-and-response with hand gestures the kids, many of them Mexican-American, resolutely refused to do), as well as an odd focus on the KKK. It was a way of frightening the kids, who mostly hadn't been out of Philly, into not wandering off ("This part of Tennessee is a national center for the KKK, and we know for a fact that there have been rallies just a mile from this farm,") as well as an all-purpose historical explanatory tool.

The next day, we had some good biscuits and gravy, heard another lecture about the KKK, and caught the plane home. I'm not sure how the summer tutoring program went.

2. *(by van)*

That summer, I got a job as a "lead counselor" for a summer camp where kids would come to a science museum for a couple days and then we'd take them on a two-night camping trip in a different state park every week. Being "lead counselor" meant I drove the 15-person van (in spite of belatedly getting my license the previous month), which was fine enough as it went, though I had a lot more trouble parking the van in the tiny parking space behind the museum, giving it another scrape or ding after every two-night trip.

The kids were almost all white boys from the suburbs who were pretty easy going and interested in digging for fossil shark teeth or going to see an owl show or whatever we did at the state parks. One time, coming down from a hike at Rickets' Glen, a 9-year-old decided he didn't want to go any further and stood there and screamed continuously like a klaxon for twenty minutes. Other than that, these were the kinds of kids for whom yelling worked.

I was subletting a nice one-bedroom from a Penn law student who'd be moving in in August. The apartment was spotless, and my friends from Americorps had mostly left when the year was up, so I'd spend a lot of time when I wasn't on the weekly camping trip lying on the floor of the apartment (I didn't have any furniture) reading, or walking all around the city by myself. One day, I ran into a sort of hip-hop white guy I knew from Americorps who told me he was now homeless and asked me if I had a place to stay. He moved in, and brought a somewhat dilapidated TV he found on the street, and sat watching TV and eating Cocoa Puffs for the next couple months. The day I had to turn in the keys to the Penn law student, he was still sleeping next to the TV at noon when I finally got him awake. He shuffled off, with his TV and his sleeping bag, and I manically wiped the walls and vacuumed the floor for the next two hours.

I think that was the day I decided to move to New York.

3.   *(Down Grand Concourse to 161st street)*
We didn't go on any field trips my first year teaching until the last week of school, when we went a few blocks south to Yankee Stadium to see the Yankees play the Red Sox. Arthur, Lavonne, Owen, almost all

the kids who'd driven me crazy all year (Franklin wasn't allowed to go on the trip) laid aside their grievances with one another to boo the Red Sox and cheer the Yanks. It was the Peaceable Kingdom, for a couple hours there in the cheap seats. I forgot to pack myself a lunch, and Danny J's silent Salvadoran mother, who remembered the water rocket I'd made with him the previous month, kept smilingly passing me one baloney sandwich after another through the seventh inning stretch.

It was a happy ending to what I was sure would be my most exhausting year.

4. *(across the street)*

My second year turned out to be much more exhausting; two thirds of my students were back, well-remembering all the insanity from the previous year; the BOE was making me go to grad school at night to keep my alternative credential, and my grad school adviser was telling me to do a variety of crazy things in my class; the school was more chaotic than the previous year, after losing two administrators at the end of the previous year and being taken over by the state; and I was just less conscientious and energetic than I had been the year before. In October, my Teach for America project director, executive director, and TFA's vice-president showed up in my class one 8th period and stood in the back of the room while 31 13-year-olds ignored both the visitors and my explanation of how sedimentary rock formation was like the plot of Apollo 13, and instead talked steadily among themselves.

One Friday in December, in sublime stupidity, I put everyone's chairs in a circle and said we were going to discuss our issues, as my grad school adviser had told me to do. This was pointless with first period, annoying with 3rd, a bad idea with 5th and 6th, and then came 8th period. Within a minute or two of sitting down and me beginning my "I notice we've had a lot of trouble focusing on our work recently, and that many of you have complained of people picking on one another" speech, Jacob had said something intolerable to Tiffany and she had stood up to start methodically punching him in the chest, while he stoically stared at the ceiling.

"Tiffany! Tiffany!" I yelled.

"He's lying about me," she said, continuing to punch. Claiming that people were lying about her was a frequent refrain from Tiffany, as I'd discovered in a recent parent conference with her mother and the vice-principal.

"I don't care what he said, just siddown!" I said.

"You don't care?" Tiffany asked, incredulous. The rest of the class began a long, low "Ooooooooohhh!"- the universal sound of middle-schoolers instigating a fight.

"Just. Sit. Down. Over there. Away from Jacob."

She sat down. "You don't care?"

A few scattered shouts- "None of these teachers care, don't you know? Just a paycheck to them." Suddenly everyone was the New York Post editorial page.

I thought I'd redirect the topic to the lesson. "Of course, your teachers and I care very much, we just want you to make the best of the opportunities you've been given."

"'Don't you care about your Education, ya lazy kids?'" someone yelled out, in a parody of a Serious Adult. Everyone laughed, and then started talking among themselves.

"Let's try to listen to each other so everyone gets a chance to talk," I tried, but everyone just talked to each other. "Listen," I said louder. Everyone still talking.

Meanwhile, Jacob was mouthing various Unforgivable Curses at Tiffany across the circle of chairs. She stood up, took a deep breath, and began rushing toward him. I jumped up and placed myself midway in her trajectory; she started pushing me towards Jacob's chair with both hands, yelling at him and me.

"Fuck you, Tiffany," I said quite clearly.

Everyone stopped talking. Tiffany looked at me, stopped pushing, and rushed out the classroom door.

I sat back down, put my head in my hands for a second, looked back up. Everyone was watching me.

"I'm very sorry for saying that to Tiffany, and for using those words."

A few scattered cries of, "we understand," and "these kids today areintolerable." Other people saying,"it's going to be a law suit!" or "you talk about uspicking on each other," and "...fired..." I looked up at the classroom clock, which was very slowly making its way to 3:20.

Beeeeeeeeeeep. Everyone rushed out, leaving the chairs in a circle. I went looking for the union rep.

"You didn't say it," the union rep said.

"I didn't say it? Everyone heard me say it. I apologized to the class for saying it."

"Look, was she cursing at Jacob? Was she saying 'I'm going to fuck you up?' or something like that?"

"Yeah, something like that."

"So you just were repeating what she said, to make sure you heard it correctly."

On Monday morning, during homeroom, the PA system came on, telling me to report to the office. Tiffany's mom was there, and the principal.

"Did you say it?"

I said what the union rep told me to say.

"He's lying about me," Tiffany said. She and her mom left.

The principal stared at me silently for a while and said, "I wouldn't get too comfortable."

The union rep found me later that day. "You'll stay until the end of the year, he'll write you a recommendation if you need one, and you'll leave." I thanked him profusely.

"Hey, don't mention it," he said. "These fucking kids, huh? They'll knock into you all day long, but as soon as you say anything, they're so damn sensitive. Just try not to slip again. And don't get in the way of any more fights."

The rest of the year became steadily less miserable and steadily more surreal. One morning, I told 8-215, "Let's go look at the moon."

"The moon ain't out, it's daytime!"

"Let's go out and look at the moon."

We went to the schoolyard and looked at the last-quarter moon.

The next day, I told them, we were going to go find some crustaceans.

"This is the Bronx, where you gonna find shrimp?"

"We going to the beach?"

We walked to the vacant lot two doors down from the school. I had seen the huge rats that lived here at night, but I figured it was safe enough during the day. Most of the kids stood along the sidewalk, while me and David L. and Jossani walked in and started flipping over the pieces of cardboard I'd left on the ground a couple hours before. All of them were covered in pill bugs, isopods.

"See," I said? "Crustaceans."

After school once or twice a week, I'd bring little groups of kids on the train down to the Natural History museum, to go see dinosaurs or the space exhibit. It was free for us to take the train, and free to get into the museum.

In class, one day in May, I brought in my guitar and tried to make up a song about the moon:

The moon is the second brightest object in the sky

after the sun

384,000 kilometers away

hey!

5. *(The big yellow schoolbus)*

My third year, at my new school, we went upstate to the state park I'd worked at on Saturdays for the previous year. My friend who ran the nature center there, just beginning to slow his speech and movement, thanks to the brain cancer that would kill him the following year, brought the kids up to the frog pond, and then found a goose that had been run over on the road going through the park and suggested dissecting it. I had been looking for spiders with a group down on the little bridges going over the lake, and we came back up to see Amy and Jack beaming, their latex gloves splattered with bright red blood, holding goose livers and hearts up to a magnifying glass.

6. *(take the Long Island Expressway)*

The next year, we decided to do an overnight trip with the whole 7th grade, and so we went way out on Long Island to an old mansion that was falling apart but had been used for school trips for the previous fifty years (this was the last year before it was shut down.) There was an aviary next to the mansion filled with hawks and eagles, and a path that went down to the shore. In a moment of great stupidity, at sunset I waded out into the water with a bunch of kids until the water was over our hips, tried to see the crabs scuttling over the rocks at our feet.

But sometimes stupidity isn't punished, and we all walked back into the beach, back up to the mansion and had dinner in the cafeteria, where we could still hear the shrieking hawks.

7. *(further on the Long Island Expressway)*

The next year, the mansion was shut down, so we went out to a real summer camp site, even further out on Long Island. A kid broke his collarbone playing baseball and lay on the ground with tears streaming down his face for what felt like hours before a nurse came and set the bone; his dad borrowed a car and showed up near the middle of the night to pick him up.

8. *(The 5 train)*

Every year, in my second school, we'd take the seemingly endless train trip from the East Village to the Bronx Zoo, and go to Jungle World (before heading to the gorillas). The gibbons would shriek at one another, and slap the tapir that lived in their enclosure on its butt, and the black leopard who looked like Bagheera, would pace back and forth exactly like in the Rilke poem:

His vision, from the constantly passing bars,
has grown so weary that it cannot hold
anything else. It seems to him there are
a thousand bars; and behind the bars, no world.
As he paces in cramped circles, over and over,
the movement of his powerful soft strides
is like a ritual dance around a center
in which a mighty will stands paralyzed.
Only at times, the curtain of the pupils
lifts, quietly–. An image enters in,
rushes down through the tensed, arrested muscles,
plunges into the heart and is gone.

9. (across the park)

A colleague and friend once left most of her students on the subway platform and went on by herself with just a few kids. Luckily, the rest of us were there (we'd come from ice-skating at the park) and could pick up the rest of the kids.

The colleague, who was young and beautiful, left the school early that year, and died early the following year, most likely of an overdose. Her mother came to the school and gave a beautiful speech to the kids about working hard at school, to remember their teacher's memory.

10. (over the bridge)

Our colleague had died two weeks before my wedding (she was good friends with my wife), and by the memorial service the word had gotten out, through a loose-lipped guidance counselor, that my wife and I (who were teaching at the same school) were married. The next day, a pencil-drawn card showing two hands– one black and one white, entwined– showed up on my wife's desk, with dozens of signatures.

11. (through the trees)

Somehow, my last year teaching, I ended up teaching AP Environmental Science. One of the required labs was a census of plants in an area. We went up and down the woods near the school, counting the species, and I kept telling the students to watch out for poison ivy and to be careful. None of them got poison ivy, I did.

12. *(down Essex st)*

R. was by any reasonable account a good looking kid, a tall, sandy-haired, sapphire-eyed 7th grader with a winning smile. He could barely read at all, and his writing, on the rare occasions I saw any of it, was a strange cuneiform of reversals and jagged dashes that was almost as painful to read as it obviously was for him to write. It probably wasn't fair to say he hated school- he seemed to like wandering behind the desks, stealing girls' pens or "misplacing" their backpacks, so they would scream at him in the mingled rage and adoration that 7th grade girls save for the really good-looking boys. And he liked paper-ball fights with his friend Abraham, another Special Ed inclusion kid, a short, round-faced, big bellied Dominican boy with a giant smile and a chortling laugh who learned almost as little in my class as R. did, apart from the time R. dared Abraham to eat the beef liver we were looking at under the microscope, and then Abraham projectile vomited onto his Special Ed teacher an hour or two later. At any rate Abraham showed up every day, while R. showed up intermittently, from time to time, as if he were attached to school by a tether that was only from time to time pulled in.

I can imagine R. now on the first day, although probably I am combining several different days-outside the class after everyone else has come in, still in the hallway, his huge red cap backwards on his head, baggy jeans too low, reciting Eminem lyrics in an undertone, to himself and me equally.

"Come on in," I said. "But no hat." R. removed the huge red baseball cap, held it in his hands in front of him, grinned at me in that loopy way, and sauntered into my class, and immediately lopped it back onto his head before going to find his seat.

I had moved- been semi-fired- from the huge terrible school in the Bronx to this tiny new hippy-dippy middle school in the East Village, not even a school really, just a couple classrooms at the end of one third floor hallway on top of some elementary schools, and I had resolved that I wasn't going to be an asshole here, was going to be a real teacher instead of some schmuck who spends his life screaming at everybody. I wasn't sure what that meant, a real teacher, though I'd spent a lot of the summer buying various little critters and setting them up in terraria, giant African millipedes and wolf spiders and land snails and huge horned beetles, and a river tank with a few kinds of fish. We were going to be real scientists, our first unit was going to be observing all these cool weird bugs I'd ordered from Carolina Biological and figuring out experiments on their behavior- did they like light colored construction paper or dark? could you teach the millipedes to climb up a ruler and did it matter if there was food at the other end? would wolf spiders prefer the bigger crickets or the smaller? that kind of thing. The principal was just a few years older than me, and he was fine with me figuring out the curriculum as I went along, as long as the parents didn't complain. The parents had more-or-less chosen him, a 5th grade teacher in one of the local elementary schools, to start the new middle school, and the local district superintendent would come to adore him, because he understood intuitively that his job was to defer decisions that would be better made by someone else.

So there I was, in this gorgeous classroom on the top floor of this Lower East Side old brick schoolhouse- and in my memory the windows all go from floor to ceiling, practically, the sun streaming in in the morning almost impossibly bright, and R. and his class came in that first sunny September day.

In the Bronx, I'd tried to sound scary and intimidating the first day, and one 8th grade girl- Naima? Natasha? I don't remember her name- who could have passed for 35 in appearance as well as attitude- drawled "why you tryin to sound like somebody you not?"

So here, in the Lower East side, I wanted to be different. I told them my name and then I gave them my #if***nglovescience speech, *avant la lettre,* circa 2002:
"A *Day Without Science is a Day without Sunshine,* because science isn't just the sun, it's not just the energy that the sun's nuclear fusion reactions produce, it's the tree that uses that energy to turn air and water into leaves and bark and wood, it's the

insect that turns that tree back into air and water and energy, or changes it into something new. It's our job as scientists not just to understand how that works, but to find out how we can *show* how it works, how we can put it to the test. So let's get started."

Some kids learned some stuff that year, and we had fun even when we didn't. Probably somewhere- in some landfill, gradually decaying if nowhere else- exist the comic books they drew based on the Jane Goodall book we read, "a Day in the Life of a wild Chimpanzee," with comparisons with the gorillas we saw when we went to the zoo, and somewhere is the gigantic painted mural of our bean plants' growth over time that was strung across the room, and the graphs of their heart rates when they jumped up and down on their chairs and then stuck their faces into bowls of cold water, and the strings we used to measure the circumference and diameter of the oak trees in Tompkins Square Park, and the illustrated anatomy of a goose that Amy and Jack dissected when we were up at Bear Mountain, upstate, on our big trip, and somewhere, sealed unchanging in some Tupperware container, is probably some of the foul-smelling pond water we kept in a closet to grow more paramecia, and somewhere are the pictures they were supposed to draw of the liver and blood cells under the microscope, that R. dared Abraham to eat.

It is a strange and potent gift to get to do the thing you are meant to do when you are still young, and I was no great teacher but I got to do what I was meant to do, for a few short years, in that room, and like Ezra Pound said:

'Thank you, whatever comes.' And then she turned
And, as the ray of sun on hanging flowers
Fades when the wind hath lifted them aside,
Went swiftly from me. Nay, whatever comes
One hour was sunlit and the most high gods
May not make boast of any better thing
Than to have watched that hour as it passed.

R. ended up in trouble with the law a few years later, in 10th or 11th grade, I think. He agreed to testify against some people involved in a robbery. He was murdered in broad daylight on a busy street in the Lower East Side. I suspect the police didn't pursue the investigation because they didn't want it to be clear that they should have protected him.

At his funeral, his cousin, another former student, a sharp-tongued, smart and funny girl, rushed to me and hugged me.

"Don't cry," she said. "He's in a better place, and at peace."

As I recall, it was an open casket funeral, the sapphire eyes closed, the smooth and handsome face well prepared by the mortician, a dark grey suit suggesting the man the boy could have grown up to be.

I remember him, before then, though, sitting in my sunny classroom, arriving having been kicked out of math or reading class, during my prep period. He is watching the few goldfish that are swimming around the "river"-style tank, the continuous gurgling whooshing sound that the kids tell me makes them need to use the bathroom more than in other classes, and telling me about the pet "Oscars" he has at home, how territorial they were and how if you put any other fish into the tank with it, it would attack. And then R. gets up, takes out that absurdly huge red baseball cap and adjusts it back on his head, and strolls back into the hallway, or somewhere else.

13.

I went with my own family to some national parks in the Southwest last Fall. On one perfect, crystalline day, we climbed around Arches National Park; through the arches you could see the snow-covered Rockies in perfect, crystalline clarity.

To see, not to learn, is in the end the purpose of every trip.

50821013R00090

Made in the USA
Middletown, DE
27 June 2019